Echoes of Eden

A Reflection on Hedonism and Happiness in the Christian life

By

Tony VC Lowe

Table of Contents

<u>Introduction</u>

John snorts a line of cocaine, drops a pill and chases it with three shots of vodka. His blood feels like lightning while the fans are cheering... he runs out onto the stage and dives into the crowd as they scream his name...

God has something better.

Manuel wakes up in a Roman villa with the taste of fine wine floating upon his breath. Francesca the underwear model glides across the room in her silken lingerie, ready to slip back into his bed. Sasha is already on his left arm. These two will be notch numbers 6 and 7 for that week...

God has something better.

Rachel jet-sets across the world. She swims with dolphins in Hawaii... she walks the great wall of China. She sees everything this world has to offer whether it be the beautiful landscapes, the magnificent buildings or all of the fascinating people inside them. She does it at her leisure; at her own pace with more money than she can spend...

God has something better.

Natalie saves a village from starvation. They were without food or proper sanitation until they were lucky enough to see her and her team. She built them wells, shops... even schools. After years of hard work she walks through a sea of smiling faces, knowing that every one of those smiles is owed to the work she did.

God has something better.

What about this: Bruce is standing in the warm embrace of Moira, who he knows is the love of his life. They have known and grown together from the beginning. After they promised to live for one-another, to love one-another in sickness or in health they had proven that promise time and time again. Now they stand watching their children play. Their eldest son Samuel has just been happily married himself after qualifying as a doctor. His first child is on the way. He helps his little sister Stephanie play a few keys on the piano. She's delighted when she gets it right. They both are. The other kids are outside playing with the dogs. Catching the sound of their laughter Bruce knows – right there – that he is so happy that he could die.

Even then... God has something better.

My priest once explained to me that serious Catholics tend to make a mistake. He explained that they often see God as an angry policeman with a rubber truncheon, ready to lay down the law whenever they do wrong. He continued to explain that, although any motivation to serve God has its value, it's an immature mindset which many need to grow out of. Instead, we have to realise that God is our loving Father. We have to remember that He cares for us; that all of His rules and strictures, however harsh they might seem, are ultimately for us and our own Good.

We need to remember this if we are to see the pleasures of this life in their full context. After all, God comes up against so many of them. Indeed, God never tells us to pursue what we enjoy in life. You could design the most enjoyable life for yourself from scratch; yet, if you offered that up to God He would say:

"pick up your cross and follow Me."[1] You could imagine the most enjoyable life possible but God tells us that we must be willing to give up this life; that we must be willing to die for Him if we are to be worthy of Heaven.

Keep in mind that the history of the saints is not full of people who did what they felt like. It is full people who gave themselves up to be eaten by lions and who wandered the desert in famine.

If you have faith – that is to say – if you have *trust* in God, you must trust that He has something better in store for you than whatever this life has to offer. If He loves you, what else would He be asking you to trade it for? But here's the rub: we'll never get our hands on what that better thing is until this life is over. That is to say, if we are willing to trade the pleasures of this life for something else, we will never really know what we're getting until we've already traded everything to get it.

This thought flowers into a number of different topics. First of all, we could ask some more questions about the nature of this trade. We must trust in God's promise of Heaven, but is this promise blind and baseless? Also, does our willingness to give up our pleasures mean that we are consigned to a life of misery? Let us not forget that the saints often bore their trials with joy. Indeed, one of the reasons that we can have trust in God's promise of heaven is that he gives us glimpses of joy in this life. It's not that God tells us *not* to enjoy anything in this life but that He insists that such enjoyment is not the full story. God has allowed for joy in this life. Yet, there are particular ways to get it. Not least, this joy may well be ever-connected to Love.

This got me thinking: we get a glimpse of Holy Love and joy through the Christian life... what kind of world could we live in if

---

1   Matthew 16:24-26

everyone strove for this? More importantly, what would this world look like *compared* to the world that's in need of it? You see, this could help bring the good that we are living for into greater relief. It can be easy to focus on the negative. God may become nothing but a policeman with a truncheon or the world may also become nothing but a miserable trial full of sin, corruption and lies. The focus can easily become a question of fighting *against* Evil instead of fighting *for* Good. But gardeners pull weeds so that the flowers can thrive.

And so, for this reflection to be complete, all of these questions will need to be answered. Hence, that is what this book intends to be. It intends to reflect on the nature of enjoyment and consider its relation to Divine Purpose. Moreover, it intends to compare lives lived in pursuit of Divine Purpose with those lived without it. Finally, it also strikes me that a final analysis is in order. To consider the nature and – dare we say – shortcomings of enjoyment might be too low of a target. Instead, couldn't we say that mere enjoyment is too hollow of a pursuit but that 'happiness' is something richer and greater that we strive for?

Faith in Joy

We don't bargain with God. There's a reason why He creates *covenants* with His people and not "deals". There is no negotiation. The terms are set and He sets them. True enough, it does appear that God "gives" things to us. If nothing else, God the Father gave us God the Son who sacrificed His own life in exchange for our salvation. This means that we do have places where we seem to find God making a kind of exchange. Yet, I'm being tentative about this because I'm not clear enough about the theology to conclude whether making God a participant in a "trade" cheapens His status in some way. As long as we have that in mind and treat the idea of a "trade" as a possible misnomer, perhaps we can still use it for the purposes of explanation.

In the opening chapter I presented the idea that there is a kind of trade that we're being offered by the Christian life. Let's take this idea further... within our own pockets we have all of the potential enjoyment that we can get out of life if we pursue our own selfish pleasures with no regard for God and His Will (unless this happens accidentally and God's Will happens to coincide with our selfish ends). On the other hand, we are presented with promises of everlasting life and bliss to enjoy for all eternity. Yet, to gain this we must be willing to sacrifice everything in this life, including life itself.

What precedent is there for this?

Firstly, there are all of the promises made about the rewards that will be received by the righteous:

"Blessed is the one who perseveres under trial because, having stood the test, that person will receive the crown of life that the Lord has promised to those who love him."[2]

---

2   James 1:12

"Blessed are the poor in spirit,

for theirs is the kingdom of heaven.

Blessed are those who mourn,

for they will be comforted.

Blessed are the meek,

for they will inherit the earth.

Blessed are those who hunger and thirst for righteousness,

for they will be filled.

Blessed are the merciful,

for they will be shown mercy.

Blessed are the pure in heart,

for they will see God.

Blessed are the peacemakers,

for they will be called children of God.

Blessed are those who are persecuted because of righteousness,

for theirs is the kingdom of heaven."[3]

Secondly, there are all of the times when He mentions the sacrifices that need to be made.

"If anyone would come after me, let him deny himself and take up his cross and follow me.[4]

"If you come to me but will not leave your family, you cannot be my follower. You must love me more than your

---

3   Matthew 5: 3-11
4   Matthew 16: 24

father, mother, wife, children, brothers, and sisters—even more than your own life!"[5]

As we can see, Christ demands everything but is willing to reward far more than that in return.

That's the trade... we are to be willing to give up everything in life, including all of our worldly pleasures and so long as we live for the sake of God, we will be rewarded with the Kingdom of Heaven; a joy which is ever-lasting. Yet, here's the rub... we know that life is full of pleasure. We experience it all of the time. We know it's full of pain too and that pain is... well... painful. Hence, we want to experience our pleasures all the more because not only do they make life enjoyable on their own merits but they serve as a respite from our suffering. We know what it's like to experience pleasure and pain in life because we are living it. Yet, none of us have ever been to Heaven[6]. None of us have direct proof of this eternal bliss with which to compare this life to. This makes the promises of Christ all the more difficult because when it comes down to it, He would have us give up something we already know; that we already rely upon for something that we have no direct experience of...

Or would He?

That's the first question that we need to think about.

Like so much in the Christian religion, the prospect of Heaven is something that we have to take on faith. Having never been there, we are putting our trust in Christ's words. Yet, is this trust – is this *faith* blind and baseless?

There are two ways to approach this question. First, it's a question of putting our trust in Christ generally. Christian faith doesn't require blind, unthinking robots. In fact, the strongest

---

5   Luke 14: 26
6   Arguably, some mystics have been rewarded with glimpses of paradise but you know what I mean.

forms of faith result from the use of reason; from sincere enquiry and even consistent tests in which Christ has proven to the faithful that following Him is the best thing for them. There are usually ups and downs in this process; times of doubt, times of reconciliation... but the point is that faith isn't a matter of accepting Christ with nothing to go on. Instead of being baseless, we often base our faith on reason, evidence and its effect on our lives. The "faith" part comes in to close the gap. Lacking omniscience, there is always a gap that we need to close when it comes to knowledge; we do this with faith. Think about any friend that you rely on. They might have helped you 99 times in the past when you have been in need. They have been so reliable that you're practically certain that when you ask them the 100th time they will do what you need. Yet, strictly speaking, you don't *know* that for sure. It *could* be the case that they don't. Instead, you simply trust that they will; you have *faith*.

What relevance does this have for joy?

The relevance is that the faithful develop a trust in Christ. It's as if, over time, His word becomes more reliable. As a result, we simply come to trust Christ as a person[7]. Now, when it comes to something like Heaven... yes, we won't technically know for sure whether Christ's promises about it are true until we get there and experience it for ourselves. But does that mean that our faith in Heaven is baseless? No. It's not baseless because our trust in Christ isn't baseless. If Christ has shown himself to be reliable 99 times, we take this extra thing on a matter of faith which has been earned. Thus, when Christ tells us to forego the pleasures in this life for His sake in order to gain something greater in the life to come, it brings the full-force of our Christian conviction to bare on whether we will trust this promise or not. The degree to which we will be willing to *risk* something – *anything* – for this promise will depend on how much trust we have.

---

7 or indeed the truth found within His Church (for the same reasons)

Then again, do we completely lack *any* experience of Heaven? This is the second way to approach the question and will be a large part of what this book is about. Enjoyment appears to play a role in the Christian life. True enough, we should be cautious about this but it does appear that God has given us our emotions for a reason (twisted and warped as they might now be)

If Heaven is our ultimate end and purpose, perhaps God hasn't left us without any indication of what this is like. After all, God *is* Goodness, Truth, Beauty and Love... a testament to this has been written into all of His creation, even if elements of that creation have strayed away from His Grace. Fallen as our world may be, echoes of Eden can be heard throughout it and perhaps God uses these echoes to speak to us; telling us about what life could and should be. Enjoyment comes in many forms and flavours in this life, from the perverse and fleeting to the lasting and sublime... our enjoyment of this life must come secondary to God's Will but perhaps it is also the case that God uses aspects of this enjoyment to tell us about His intentions for us in the World to Come.

And so, what is the nature of the trade?

On the one hand, we have all of the pleasures and comforts that we can selfishly enjoy within this life. On the other hand we have God, who doesn't tell us that all of our pleasures *will* be stripped away the moment we become Christian but who does say that we should be *willing* to hand our pleasures over to embrace a life of pain for His sake. In return, we will gain a new level of enjoyment; a place in Heaven which will make the pleasures and comfort of this life seem like cabbage soup. We wouldn't make this trade blindfolded with a complete stranger, nor do we. Instead, we can make this trade with open eyes. We can trust in the exchange because we trust that God is trustworthy and not only this, but we may also find places where

God has sprinkled examples – where He has given us *samples* – of the Heavenly as a fore-taste of what He intends to give us if we are willing to pay the price.

Cold Heaven

Is enjoyment the thing that proves the truth of Christianity? No. One shouldn't become a Christian because it feels good, nor should they reject it because they find it to be unpleasant.

According to the book of Revelation, God declares that a person can either be hot *or cold* but if you are lukewarm He will spit you out of His mouth.[8] We can leave the question of lukewarmness aside but focus on the fact that one can remain "cold" and rest in the arms of God. We cannot exhaust the meaning of this statement here but we can understand that "coldness" can pertain to a particular kind of relation to God; namely, an emotionless one. Yes, humans are seldom – if ever – unfeeling robots but the idea here is that people can have a belief in God and live a good Christian life independently of their feelings about it. Even within a whirlwind of lifelong pain we can still have clear conviction in Christ because of our faith.

Therefore, we don't need emotions to believe in God but do we leave them out of the picture? This doesn't appear to be wise either because God appears to have given us emotions for some reason. Twisted and fallen as they are, our emotions can still perceive good in particular circumstances. We can perceive the morality in the sacrifice of one stranger for another or in the glint of a beautiful sunrise. These are things that we can grasp with the mind but these things are informed by our emotions too.

Now, we also need to be clear that now that having fallen short of Eden, Heaven is the place that contains the kind of life that God really intends for us. Everything that we live through before the second coming is but a trial before that final reward. In light of this, the question is: should we presume that heaven is an emotion-less place? Or is it more intuitive and simply more likely to assume that our life in Heaven will be a place where we feel as well as think? In fact, would

---

8   Revelation 3: 15-17

we not presume that Heaven would consist of some depth of emotion that we don't even have the ability to contemplate here on earth? It's difficult to say definitively. But another thing we could consider is whether Heaven merely consists of a cold, factual, rational knowledge of God. Is that idea difficult to conceive? If it is, it may simply be more sensible to presume that God has given us our emotions as yet another way to speak to us and that joy is the voice that He uses. This is riddled with all kinds of problems and I wouldn't suggest that we should "think" with our emotions. However, that is a topic that could merit its own work. It is not the present topic of this one.

If we don't just think in Heaven but feel it, feeling has the potential to contain something which speaks of the presence of God. And lest we are to presume that *all* emotions that we experience in life are ungodly, we can presume that some of those emotions speak to Him; His presence, His purpose and the kind of life that He intends for us to live.

Samples of Heaven

To get a really clear idea of what enjoyment entails in life we have to make separate distinctions between a number of different things including love, pleasure, joy, happiness… yet, these distinctions are the kinds of things that we are trying to draw-out in the course of this book. To say what "true" happiness is compared to mere pleasure won't be clear before we consider the different ways that people approach both or where their shortcomings might be. As a result, a full exposition of what true joy is compared to enjoyment in general is best saved until the end.

Still… where are we standing here at the start? When we posit the question of whether God speaks to us through our enjoyment of life, what possibly comes to mind?

First, we could start with the moments which are explicitly related to The Faith.

The examples that come to mind are those moments when people attest to a consolation from God in their troubles… perhaps they feel His presence in some numinous way or have "felt" Him talking… In particular, I am reminded of the examples of St. Teresa of Avila who wrote about times during her long contemplative prayers when God would afford her moments of peace[9], or when St. Thomas Aquinas received a vision of Heaven, compared to which he realised that his entire life's work was "straw"[10]. I am reminded of the stories of numerous other Saints who found peace in the desert[11] or sang with joy, even unto the moment of death.[12] This case of St. Thomas is pertinent because it is – of course – a literal sample of Heaven given to us here on earth. Hence, when we are to ask whether God gives us an idea of the

9   *Letters* of St. Teresa of Avila
10   *Saint Thomas Aquinas: The Dumb Ox* by G.K. Chesterton
11   https://www.britannica.com/biography/Saint-Anthony-of-Egypt
12   http://faith.nd.edu/s/1210/faith/interior.aspx?
     sid=1210&gid=609&pgid=46478&cid=89095&ecid=89095&crid=0&calp
     gid=61&calcid=53508

life to come, whether He makes His presence explicit to us or gives us a glimpse of Heaven, it is another thing that supports His promises.

What, then, of things that don't pertain to The Faith? If we are to take a broad view of those parts of life that we enjoy, which can we say speak to our path to Heaven? This is of course far more difficult to say. At the very least, I believe that common intuition would give us a starting point... we would, for example, recognise that watching TV gives us pleasure of an altogether different quality from beholding a majestic sunrise or that a rush of cocaine is a feeling less "pure" than beholding the light in your child's eyes. Indeed, there are many people – religious or not – who have been fortunate enough to find moments in which everything seems right with the world; in which they are perfectly content in every way... a state which we might refer to as "bliss". And so, we know that bliss can occur. Yet, we can also recognise that it tends to be fleeting. Beyond this, pleasure and pain are so intermingled within life and have so many different gradations that it's hard to say which elements speak of God.

That's why it seems like a good place to proceed is into the Christian life. At the very least, God has not allowed life in our fallen state to be completely unenjoyable, nor does this happen to the Christian life. The question would then be: does the experience of enjoyment change as the Christian life is implemented? This seems to be central to our enquiry because it will allow us to distinguish between the enjoyment which we happen upon and the way in which life might become more enjoyable if we live it as Christians; by doing what God has told us to do. If doing what God has told us to do makes elements of life more pleasant, it is these elements that would speak to His intentions for our enjoyment more than anything else.

The Christian Life

I am a Catholic[13]. This is relevant because what Catholics take for the 'Christian' life is simply the Catholic life; they are one and the same. Hence, when making a sketch of the Christian life in this section of the book, I will be drawing upon the Catholic model. This is not to isolate this work from the consideration of others who consider themselves Christian. My guess is that others who consider themselves to be Christian yet not Catholic will find a great deal of overlap between their understanding of the Christian life and the one presented here. Indeed, this overlap may be so substantial that it makes them regard the Catholic distinction as superfluous. However, the distinction needs to be made because if there are various models of the ideal Christian life (which there are), one needs to be prioritised if we are to speak about it. Therefore, it is worth being clear about which one is being prioritised from the outset.

Catholicism is far from monochromatic; it's members and Saints have lived wildly different lives which have been vibrant and full of colour. Yet, it is also the case that there is an agreed upon model for a Catholic life; agreed upon rules that bind us to God's Will and His Church. It is these rules that set the basic model for Catholic life which are mostly found in Catechism.

However, I will try not to focus on the administrative parts of Catholic life such as recognising the hierarchy of Bishops or submitting to the Pope. These things are important[14] but for the current reflection I am less interested in how a given person

---

13 In fact, I hold to the position of Sedevacantism or Sedepriviationism. Those who are familiar with these terms will understand this entails a large, serious argument which I will not be addressing here. Still, I must be clear about my position.

14 Indeed, they are essential.

relates to Church structure than I am in how that person lives their life day to day whilst they are part of that Church.

And so, what does the Christian life consist of? Broadly speaking, here are a few things that come to mind...

> Belief in God,
> A willingness and indeed a resolve to live by His commandments, which means -amongst other things- no stealing, no adultery, no slander or false witness, no envy or lust for what others have and no [unjust][15] killing,
> An emphasis on living through and beyond this life as if we are living in preparation for something greater to come,
> Loyalty, commitment and the support of one's family,
> A general eagerness to give mercy and forgive,
> A general eagerness to do one's work and to do it well,
> A general feeling of gratitude for what one has and bitter-less acceptance for what one lacks,
> A general wariness of money and an understanding that it is only ever a means to an end, not something that should be loved as an end unto itself,
> Love of one's neighbour.

There are many other elements pertaining to the Christian life too, including relations to authority, relations within families, prayer, the life of the mind and so on. Some of these elements, including those listed, will be drawn out in the examples below, though some may not. In any case, it has been useful for us to have a sketch of the Christian life and its ideals.

---

15 The word original commandment "thou shalt not kill" is in fact "thou shalt not *murder*".

Idealistic?

We can also point to times in history when Catholicism was at its height to find examples of the Catholic life, but then it occurred to me that these examples will also be lacking. Indeed, have we ever seen all of the virtues listed above exemplified across a whole society at any time in history? We might point to isolated examples such as the Saints, but could we ever point to a town or city that was as Christian as it *could* be? The answer is no. But that's not the point. We are fallen beings in a fallen world with a fallen nature. We are in a constant state of war between the City of Man and the City of God and this war reverberates throughout every level of our being; from the internal, right through to the political. Hence, we should never expect there to be a society which exemplifies Christian virtue.

The list given above is an aspiration, not a reality. Yet, that makes it no less important. Imagine an archer who needs to hit his target, but who finds that every time he aims for it he is 10 meters short of the mark. And so, what does he do? He doesn't aim for that target. Instead, he aims at another one which is 10 meters above it. What he finds is that he misses this second target above, but by trying to do so, he is finally able to hit the one that was below. This is a rough analogy but hopefully it illustrates the idea: the standards which God has given us to aspire to are like a target drawn in Heaven that we are almost never going to hit in this life. Yet, if we keep our aim held high, we might hit the target which is drawn for us here on earth. If we take all of the Christian virtues together, there is almost no-one who exemplifies all of them. They might have 4 of 5 virtues, or 9 of 10, but all of us fall short of the mark in some way. For this reason we could say that the truly Christian life has not been realised in full on earth, nor will it ever be. It has not been a reality, yet, that is not to say that it is not *realistic*... instead, it simply has not been realised. Instead, it is an ideal to strive for until it is attained, even if we chase it unto eternity.

And so, will this book drawn a picture of Christianity which is idealistic? Yes. We always fall short of the mark. But that's not the point. The point is to get a clearer idea of what hitting the mark means and what that would entail. 'Hitting the mark'[16] is what God intends for us and so realising these virtues is also what He intends for us. Hence, if we are to consider the life that He intends with the enjoyment that it entails, we should take the picture in its ideal form.

A Christian Monopoly on the Good Life?

The assumption is that this book will appeal to a Christian audience and so this question will only be visited briefly... if we consider the list of virtues above, do the Christians[17] claim a monopoly on such virtues and their fruits? After all, don't we find ideals such as loyalty, hard work and aversion to stealing in non-Christian societies?

There are two points to make.

Firstly, not exactly. If we are consider western nations at the least, the moral substructure of these societies is based on our Christian heritage, whether secularist atheists like it or not. Many western atheists will hold to ideals such as the right to property and the sanctity of life but frankly it is *not* because these people have reasoned about these matters form first principles. They might do so in an ad-hoc fashion, but in most cases they have these ideals because they were soaked into them as a result of their societal zeitgeist and its Christian heritage. After this, an atheist will likely play moral catch-up for their ideals using non-Christian arguments.

---

16 In ancient Greek, the word for "Sin" that is most often used in the New Testament is the Greek word "harmartia", from the root "hamartanein"; an archery term which means to "to miss the mark". Hence, if God wants us to be rid of sin, He really does want us to hit our mark.

17 Or strictly speaking, *God.*

Second, even when we consider non-Christian societies, they may well idealise some of the Christian virtues, but not all of them and that is important. You see, you cannot compare pictures of what God intends and what He does not unless you use the full picture. If a society idealised loyalty and hard work but allowed stealing, something would be missing. To put it very simply, we will consider the Christian set of morals because only Christianity contains that set of morals in its entirety.

Houses of Man, Houses of God

In Saint Augustine's *The City of God* a comparison is drawn between a Godly city that seeks to serve the ends of Heaven and a city which seeks only to serve the earthly goals of Man. Bringing this work to mind is inescapable for this section because it will seek to do something similar, though far more provincial. Instead of comparing cities, this section will compare houses. It will look at some individual examples and make a comparison. On the one hand, the person will be living with God in their lives. On the other, they will live without Him.

The idea is to use these examples to try and bring the benefits of the Christian life into greater relief. Again, this book is working with the premise that there is some way in which God uses the Christian life to show that He intends what is best for us. By comparing Christian and non-Christian lives, perhaps we can get a clearer picture of what "best" means. What's more, perhaps these examples can give us a better understanding of the role that our enjoyment plays in our lives; what forms does it take? How do we prioritise it and what does it teach us?

These examples will not appear completely realistic but that's okay because the point isn't to be realistic so much as it is to draw particular features of these lives more clearly, just as a cartoonist might. Although, it should also be mentioned that these examples are drawn heavily from real life and in many cases will be far less cartoonish than they might appear. Still, we are comparing ideals, not strict realities. As just one example, one could argue that many of the trials of Christian life are overlooked in the examples below but that's because Christian life is so intermingled with the life of this world which, as a result of the fall, is *not* what God intends for our best interests. And so, hopefully, with each example we can see more clearly the kinds of lives that God did not intend for us and those that He did.

Consider Carol

Carol sits alone drinking wine in her five bedroom house. She sits at her laptop scrolling through the Facebook messages between her husband James and his new mistress, Vicky. Carol feels jaded by this point. The emotional maelstrom wasn't nearly as intense this time as it had been on the first occasion when she caught him cheating. It was so easy too... leaving his Facebook open... *does he even care about getting caught?* Anyway, she was almost calm. The quality was different, though. She felt heavier this time; dull... instead of being tossed up by a wind, a storm was blowing but a great stone kept her suck to the ground.

Weight... that hollow feeling... was it James? No. It was the bigger picture. This wasn't the first time James had cheated but this wasn't her first husband either. Were they *all* useless, disloyal animals? Then her conscience whispered: "you're no angel." And it was true. She'd cheated her fair share of times. But she had more excuses than James: those were younger days; life was more careless, she was more immature; the stakes weren't so high... James should know better. She sighed, if only on the inside. Still, she knew what she would do. Perhaps this time was less tumultuous because it required far less thinking. Once again, she would re-shuffle the deck; find another man... or perhaps it was finally time to be alone.

Her thoughts turned to her children. What would they think? Not much. James wasn't their father and they could always adapt to the change. They always did. Besides, they were getting older now. No, instead her thoughts turned to something else... what did this life have in store for them? What kind of people would they meet and what kind of people would they be? David had a way with the ladies. Would he be a loyal, loving husband to his wife? Maybe. But if he *could* cheat? If he *could* get away with it...? And what about Jessica? Beautiful, no doubt. And a high achiever. Would she be lucky enough to find a good man? A loyal, strong, trustworthy man to father her children? But then another thought struck her: is that the kind of man that Jessica would even *want?* Or did she have something else in mind? Would Jessica look for *love?* She was beautiful and she knew how to use it... she was ambitious and she knew how to get what she wanted... she may well get married for many reasons but love might not be one of them. And if her powerful, successful husband *did* cheat, would she even care? Or would she simply factor it in? Jessica didn't live for love. Somehow Carol knew that she was too selfish for it. She had always been so single-minded... Carol always justified it as her "strong independence" but how many times had Jessica refused to help, even with little things? The time when she sat on her phone as her mum struggled with shopping or that time she rushed out for the weekend to get drunk the moment they needed someone at home when her brother was taken ill. This time Carol sighed aloud.

She looked around at her house. She had been ambitious; a real career-driven go-getter; she beheld her reward: a big house in a nice suburb; a couple of cars outside the garage (four wheel drive)... she went to the theatre on the weekend and took a trip to Tuscany in the spring... *she even had a wine rack.* Yet, that feeling still persisted. She had that dull, hollow feeling and not one thing in this house could fill it. In fact, she tasted the wine in her glass. Even before she had caught James cheating she had noticed something: the taste was simply "okay". It wasn't bad wine; it was good. She knew it was good. The first time that she had sampled a bottle like this, she couldn't believe that something could taste so luxurious. But she had become used to the taste after so many bottles and now the wine was simply... "okay". Then it struck her: the house was simply "okay". Yes it was nice and objectively speaking, it was even beautiful... but she remembered the first moment when she walked in and saw the kitchen and the garden... she remembered the first time she drove the car with its air-con and surround-sound speakers... she remembered the first time she took a plane to Europe... every time she had done these things since then, the pleasure was never quite the same. She had become callused to it. The only time she ever felt more pleasure was when she *escalated*; when she bought better wine, drove better cars, booked nicer holidays... but all of that took...

Work. The more things she wanted to enjoy, the more work she had to put in to get them and as she climbed the ladder, those promotions became harder and harder to get. How long had she worked for? A couple of decades as an accountant. It was good money. It was a respectable career. She had built a financial safety net for herself by her mid-20s and had been painting her ambitions on top of it ever since. But what had that career consisted of? Numbers, phone-calls and computer screens. One desk and four walls. The regular trips she took to the gym and Pilates classes were to stop her body from seizing up after all of that sitting down. *Decades*. And that was for 40 hours a week, *every week* for that entire time. How much time did she get for herself? How much time did she spend with her children? And now they were grown-up... almost ready to leave... almost ready to do the same thing.

It was after this cascade of thought that Carol no longer felt the weight tying her down. Now she felt it as a dead weight upon her chest. If that was it... decades spent sat in a box moving from one martial charade to the next... all the while, the flavours of life slowly fading upon her tongue... if that was it, *what was it all for?*

Carol prepares dinner one evening as James comes home from work. It had been a long day but he seldom dragged it into his home. He was happy to be there and in fact, however hard the work would get, he never begrudged it. He touches his wife on the shoulder, kisses her on the cheek and tells her that he loves her. She sighs... and it's a gentle feeling.

"I'm just serving up" she says and he smiles as he calls David to the table along with the rest of the children; Brandon, Rachel, Mary and Luke. No need to call for Jessica; she was already helping her mother. They sit around the table as James says grace, thanking God for his meal, his wife and their children. Carol says her own little "thank you". She watches as her family enjoys the work of her hands, exchanging the stories of their day. Danny had met a young woman at the Church. He almost blushed when he spoke of her, but James coaxed his son to be more forthright. They knew the young woman in question and were delighted that the spark had finally been lit. Carol and her husband encouraged their son to spend more time in Church so that they could get to know each other more. Danny was eager to do so. James emphasised that Danny should carry on being honest, respectful, *courageous* and to always put God first. They assured him that if she was a girl worth marrying, she would do the same and everything would go well. Carol felt confident that it would.

Jessica nursed her own thoughts of finding a husband and longed for the day; to share that love and have the chance of raising children of her own. She had spent so much time with her own family growing up that she knew what kind of joy that could give to a child. They had taught her, supported her, loved her and strengthened her. She couldn't wait to do the same. Carol couldn't wait for her daughter to experience that either. After she had found the solid support of James, raising her children had been the most fulfilling part of her life. Yes, it was very stressful at times, plus she was always busy, but every time she heard them say a first word or took a first step or every time she taught them something new... bliss.

The marriage to James was a bit worrying at first. He was known in the community as a hard-working, pious man (as a bonus, he was very handsome) but she knew that she couldn't be the only one with eyes for him. Even as they set their engagement she feared that some great beauty would swoon in and sweep him away. Little did she know that James *had* been coaxed by the temptation. He had been quite popular with women and at one time, he even met a young woman who came onto him in a very forward way. But he kept true. Despite the immaturity of his youth, he had always had the idea of purity soaked into him by his parents. Besides... if he ever did slip he would have to tell his priest... he dreaded the thought, let alone what would happen if the people at the Church found out that he had been so foolish! Yet, in the end it wasn't fear that stayed his mistakes. Once he had committed to Carol and understood that their commitment was before God and for life, he discovered that his love for her was something to be nurtured on a daily basis. At first came the carnal attraction of youth but by the time their first child was born it had transformed: they were now his home; his love; his care. When he first looked into Jessica's eyes he knew that he would do anything for her and the mother who made her possible. After years of commitment their love had solidified. It was no longer as vaporous as their emotions; it had become something beyond that... first they had shared each other's bodies, now they were *of one body*.

Carol looked around her house. It was simple, but she liked that. The car was simple too but it had enough seats for the kids. So long as she could take them to the park or the beach from time to time, what else did they need? Looking around the home, she didn't so much see 'things' but *memories*... there was the place where Mary had started crawling... there was where Luke had built his little Castle... and there was where Rachel had been sick all over the floor... the pantry was simple; she had the odd packet of biscuits and a bottle of wine but she was glad of it. Wine was something that she used to compliment a meal or host a guest; it was a prop in her life; something to compliment the general aesthetic but something that was never in the foreground enough to be missed. To tell the truth, she never sought pleasure in "pleasure". It was to be found somewhere else... could she even call it "pleasure"? Between the hugs from her husband and the laughter of her children "pleasure" seemed a bit too thin. No, her life was full of something more...

Commentary

What can these two examples tell us about the role of enjoyment in Christian life? Of course, the clearest hallmark of a life which is devoid of God is a life which is full of sin. It would be a step too far to call Carol *wicked* or to say that her life is *full* of sin but at the very least, we see in the first example that she lives in a milieu which surrounds her with it. Yet, of course, she is not guiltless and shares in this sin herself.

Beyond this, a distinctive feature of Carol's example is the theme of vacancy. The assault of sin is one thing but riding alongside this is a life which is hollow in a deep way. For Carol, she finds that her life is hollow when she reflects on what all of her achievements and possessions have really amounted to. In essence, the pleasures that she has worked so hard for are – at best – a diminishing return. Like a very drawn out addiction she has to earn ever more money to buy ever more elaborate pleasures to keep her satisfied. This is probably one of the most striking features of a life lived in pursuit of hedonism which is in stark contrast to a life given over to God. Chasing happiness or – at least – *pleasure* for the sake of pleasure appears to be a fool's game because the moment you have your hands on it, it shrinks and fades. Yet, its not as if the pleasures of life have no place in it. That's why we see them in the example of Carol's Christian life. In that life her cars, her home and her wine are all things to be enjoyed but they find their proper place. In many cases they are simply a pleasant means to achieve something more important but are not the end-in-themselves. Hence, we must consider that God has given us the option to pursue the things of this world. Yet, He has hidden a lesson in this choice: if we pursue Him and make His will our goal, these pleasures will be a pleasant addition to life. However, if we don't make His will our goal but set these pleasures above it we will not get what we want. We will find that the pursuit of pleasure is a hollow promise.

In the Christian example, Carol pursued something more important than pleasure and in particular, that 'something' is her family. The family is central to both examples. In the first case we see that Carol has a broken family life. Her husband is just one example in a series of failed relationships and this has an effect that cascades onto her children. From the example of her mother, they have less trust in the efficacy of long-term relationships themselves and the investment they make on connecting with a father-figure in the household is progressively deteriorated (yet, we should never forget that her children remain free agents with the choice to change). Carol made her own mistakes but even if we argued that her broken relationships were a result of failed men with bad intentions that still stresses the value of Christian life. As we saw in her Christian example, Christian society exerts a moral pressure on the men and women within it to be loyal to one-another. In modern secular society we can be lackadaisical about commitment and even have an aversion to it if it promises anything less than perpetual serenity to those involved. Yet, what this results in is far from an ideal state. Instead, it trivialises the moral standards of long-term relationships. Carol and her partners have a history of picking and choosing, of playing and cheating. Other than a vague appeal to harm, if this serves their convenience why should they not? Under Christian morality, marriage is sacramental; a Holy Bond marked by God.

This cascades onto their children. Unless the children resist the influence of their parents, they will learn from these patterns that relationships really are trivial or, at the least, they will learn to keep guarded against the idea that proper commitment is worth pursuing.

However, is family not a thing "of this world" ...? Not exactly. Yes, we live with our family here and now and may well be separated from them come the Final Judgement but even while we are here, family life involves something more eternal than material possessions. Each person in the family has a soul and in the example of Carol, we would say that by engaging in her family life she was partaking in Love. We are taught that Love is an attribute of God and is therefore eternal by its nature. Even if our interaction with Love during life is fleeting, it is an interaction with the eternal and divine. What's more, when we Love another and care for their souls, we are are sharing in that divine, eternal interaction with that divine and eternal part of them. It is not for nothing that Love is so esteemed within the Christian tradition and thank God that it is so often enjoyable. True enough, Love isn't defined by its enjoyability; modern romanticism[18] would have us believe that but in truth, Love is more akin to a choice than a feeling. It is an attitude of wanting what is best for another, even if you don't like that person. After all, we are taught to Love our enemies; to want what is best for those we like the least. Still, Love can be deeply enjoyable. When Carol Loves her children and gets time to nurture that Love in their company, and especially when her children return her smiles, care and affection the joy is undeniable.

What does the example of Carol tell us? It tells us that when we pursue a life devoid of God and seek worldly pleasure, we are grasping at a kind of fulfilment which is subject to decay; our pleasures only dry up with time lest we constantly try to resurrect them with more and more effort. What's more, it tells us that when we live in a life of sin, those aspects of life which promise to give us something deeper such as our close family connections become tainted and unreliable, unable to give us that deeper fulfilment that we seek. On the other hand, we see that if we do live the Christian life in the way that it is intended to be lived, the

---

18 Really, the romantic movement came about in the 18th century and this is when we saw an emphasis on emotion, sensuality, subjectivity and spontaneity which effected the romantic idea of love which has apparently bled into the modern day. www.britannica.com/art/Romanticism

pleasures in life find their proper place. It is as if God says "Enjoy this wine while you live for Me and you can enjoy it forever... enjoy this wine for its own sake and it will turn to dust in your hands." Aside from being cruel, this is a way of God teaching us to prioritise the valuable things in life and He makes this easier by ensuring that the things that aren't meant to satisfy us don't. Instead, the life He intends is full of deeper things like Love and family connection and if kept away from sin, these things have the time to deepen and flourish through Love and loyalty. It's as if God is saying "treat relationships in anyway you please and they will become trivial and cheap... approach them in the way I've intended and they might be hard but they will give you a kind of joy which is more pure and lasting." And so, in these two ways we seem to get some idea of how God uses joy and the *thing* that we *enjoy* to point us towards His Love.

Consider Ricky

Ricky hits a bong... stares out of the window of his council flat. He puts it down, moves his hand to the speaker... turns it up. The hard pulse of drum and bass dominates the sound of bickering growing next door. It energises him, catalysing the half can of monster energy drink chasing down his weed. He thinks to the argument next door; how he'd like to kick them both in if they ever tried anything on him. He could too; he knows it. He would hit *him* first – right under the jaw - drop him quickly. Maybe kick him a few times. That would shock her into silence for a second but a couple of slaps around the cheeks should make sure she stays that way. That would shut them up. But did that even matter? A bit. But it would also show a couple of people that he wasn't someone on the estate that they could fuck around with.

He was so angry. The thought of fighting his neighbours rode a wave of thoughts about his boss. He had woken at the crack of dawn yesterday to do a 12 hour shift which was only supposed to be 8. There was no planning and they hadn't even sorted the proper materials. Even after the 12 hours the job hadn't been done properly and the client gave him an earful. The boss had called him afterwards to check how things went. Not even a "thank you"; just moaned about the job not being finished. Ricky tucked in a question about his payslip and the boss said he'd get an extra £100 to make up for the long day. Ricky looked at his account when he got home... £50 *short* of what he'd expected. Furious, he tried to give the boss a call. Nothing. And still nothing days later. He could kill him; stomp his head to the curb... but too much of a risk. If the police caught on... that would be *it* for a long time...

But did it even matter? He thought over what he was going to do with his day and the thought lasted about 10 seconds. He looked out of his window over a greying English sky. Danny would come over in a bit. They could do a couple hits and play a bit of FIFA. Might go to the pub later... or drop a call to Lianne... see if he could get his end away... that was about it. He wasn't going back into work on Monday, that was for sure. Would he look for more work? What was the need? Everything he did was either too hard or too boring. He was always tired. And in any case, the bosses always found a way to shaft him. Besides, there was no *need*. The council didn't have time to chase him about his rent and he'd get plenty of benefits to pay for the bills. He had a bit of weed that he could sell out of his drawer so that usually kept him sorted for his fags and the odd night out. The council *might* chase him for money at some point but when that time came, he would go down to the job centre and explain the situation. No need to worry.

If a specialist ever had the time to put a term to it, they might say that Ricky was depressed. He would revile that term around his mates, but there were times when it could be useful.

Ricky's life is a dull, uninteresting, slightly uncomfortable blur. He has no ambitions, no desire and no clear incentive to become anything or do anything. Life around him mostly remains the same. He visits family and they chat about local things, do a bong, have a beer, watch a bit of TV... he sees his mates and they do the same. He sits at home, hits a bong, watches a bit of TV... and if he ever finds a girlfriend they usually do the same... What does it all amount to? What is his life for? He has a vague idea that he should be happy or feel some kind of fulfilment. Or at least, he knows that's what he desires. Instead, he fights a daily war of attrition against the grey and his main weapon in that war is the repetitive pleasures that make the grey that little bit more colourful.

There's another option that adds *colour* too: crime. It's dangerous stuff and he doesn't do it as much as he used to but the next time he gets into a fight or breaks into a car it will be so vitalising that it will virtually pull the sun[19] out from behind the clouds. The only issue was getting caught. The crime itself was never really a problem. Sure, he wouldn't steal a pint of milk out the fridge of little old Glenda, but everyone else? Who cares. He'd met most of the people on the estate and they were all lazy, spiteful, lying cheating bastards anyway. They would just as soon do it to him if they could too, so who cares?

But what did it matter anyway? Today he didn't feel like doing anything. Now that the rush of anger had burned out and the caffeine had subsided, the weed rolled in. He felt tired. Again. Time to go for a nap, and wait for something to happen...

Things are a bit hard on the estate. The economy is taking a hit and people are feeling a pinch. Ricky wants to be cautious and so he puts a few extra hours in at the yard. By the end of the first week he sees that his boss is struggling a lot but he tries to be as open with his employees as he can: "No need to pull the extra hours next week Rick, I might not be able to pay it..." he explains. When the time rolled around, Ricky decides to put the extra hours in anyway without any charge. When he checks his payslip, he find that the hours have been paid anyway. He calls his boss to check if he's misunderstood but the boss insists that *a worker deserves his wages* and that settles the matter in peace. Ricky felt grateful. He makes sure to spare a prayer for the business.

When he returns home that night to start his weekend, he find that the couple next door has prepared him dinner. He had just finished doing up one of their bedrooms because she was expecting a baby. Ricky is happy for them and gives them both

---

19 Or the moon.

his blessing. He offers to cook them dinner one day and they look forward to it. It was a little tradition that they had formed and it oscillated between them.

This weekend he'd been called out to help one of his mates find a bike that had been nicked from his lawn. A group of them went out and found that Bryson had it stashed and was intending to sell the wheels. The group of them are strict in their seizure of the bike and reprimanded Bryson on the spot for his actions but there is enough of them to hold him back from violence and when they leave him they discuss the situation further. Clearly, Bryson was in a desperate position and was clearly developing a drug habit. That was no justification for his actions but perhaps they should keep an eye on him and see if there was some way to offer a hand. They decide that each of them would visit Bryson… maybe once a day… they could cook him a meal or just give him a bit of company, or even find something for him to do. It was good to find some way to be helpful; it kept a person's mind off of things. They could speak to the priest too but all of that would come in its own time. Meanwhile, it was important for them to show him goodwill and see if there was some way to work him out of this rut.

Ricky thought of his own temptations to steal. What about that time when he'd found John's wallet on the pavement? No one would know that he took it. There was a couple hundred quid in there… but *God would know*… besides, as he learned later that that wasn't the point. Yes, God would know but as he got older he learned the value of a day's wage and began to understand that he had no right to steal that from someone else. What about the time when he'd almost decided to jump Stephen? Ricky knew he could. He'd torn through enough sparring in the boxing ring. Stephen had been bad-mouthing Ricky at work, spreading all kinds of lies about his personal life. And then one day Ricky learnt that he'd been sleeping with Lianne; the girl that Ricky had just been starting to date. Ricky was furious. But when he was on his way to ambush Stephen on his way home from the pub, the fury subsided. The sins of Stephen and Lianne were their own and she had simply proven that she wasn't a woman worth being with. Stephen required justice but when everyone else find out about his behaviour they took him to task for it... hard. He changed his actions after that. There was a time for violence: if something were to ever happen at home; a friend was in immediate danger or a family needed to be defended against am attacker... of course.

That evening Ricky goes to visit his parents, helps his mum with garden, see something that his dad is making in his workshop and then sits down for a chat about the news on the estate. The general picture is that people were chipping in to keep things afloat. Moira and Dez had their fence blown down and so Paul had popped round to fix it. Deborah's boiler had packed up and so John brought Andy round to sort it out. Wherever there was more work to be found, word got around and a lot of the older blokes were trying to bring a lot of the young men into the trade. Church was good for this because after the service they would often exchange news about jobs they found and vacancies that were coming up for the week. Ricky's mum had spoken to Andy and apparently they had a bit more plumbing work that he could get his hands on. They'd pay well too. Ricky would have to speak to his boss but when he explained the boss saw no problem. He knew Ricky worked hard and was reliable. He wasn't trying to cause the boss any problems but the boss was happy to support him as he tried to forward his prospects. "You need more money to get yourself set for a family, lad." he explained. "Don't worry about me mate. Yeah, we've lost a bit of money in the yard but let's be honest, if I own a yard I'm hardly scrounging. I've got enough to get by. There's more important things than money after all..."

Ricky's life is a bright, colourful, crystalline picture of things to come. Yes, he's moving through hard times but he feels confident in the fact that everyone around him has pulled together to lessen the blow. In fact, if he reflected on it for some time he would realise that he was almost grateful for the hard times for that very fact; it revealed the latent character of the community and once everyone had a chance to prove their worth in a time of struggle, it brought everyone closer together. He wouldn't be a rich man but if things kept going this way he would have enough money to support himself, a wife and -God willing- some children. And even if that job fell through... well, reliable friends were the kind of thing that you couldn't place a price on. There had been times when he'd felt bitter in his life and willing to do his worst against others but as time drew on he learnt that they were but ships in the same storm that he sailed.

Ricky understands that life is a struggle and a trial but he knows what that trial for and why it must be overcome. And he thanks God every day for having so many people around him that make that challenge easier to face.

Commentary

The first example of Ricky's life shares one strong parallel with Carol's: vacancy. Whereas Carol's was a life of pleasure-seeking and career building which had not afforded her the life she wanted, Ricky's is a life which hasn't gone anywhere simply because it hasn't started. Where Carol's pleasure-seeking was a striving for every more enjoyment or chasing the next proverbial "high", Ricky's is an endless attempt to use his pleasures to maintain a baseline level of enjoyment which is constantly fading. Like Carol, the pleasures that Ricky chases will never give him fulfilment and for the same reason: that's not what they are designed for.

Like Carol, Ricky lives within a milieu of sin. The fact that his bosses are so ready to underpay him and make his working life so unjust is only one of the reasons why Ricky is so devoid of motivation to strive for something better; why *should* he work hard when the world gives him no reason to do so? Hollow pleasure might be hollow but for people like Ricky, it remains preferable to thankless work. Otherwise, there are the people around him. Ricky's intentions towards all of them are apathetic at best, if not often malicious and because all of them live lives of sin, to his mind they aren't worthy of any charity. Aside from his own inertia, the only thing keeping him from abusing them for his own gain is the threat of fear from people like the police.

Yet, again, Ricky is not guiltless. Many of the malicious thoughts stem from himself and he is willing to fuel them as they arise. His attitude is not one of "they are bad, I am trying to be good" but "They are *just as bad as me."* What's more, all of his moral attitudes relate to himself. Aside from some vague idea that it's wrong to hurt old women, there is no clear idea of why honest work is good for its own sake or why being a criminal is wrong in-and-of-itself. Instead, he can only judge these things in relation to his own comfort and gratification.

What happens when we consider Ricky living in a Christian environment?

The first thing to note is that we can accept that such an environment will not be without its hardships. This time, people generally have less money. However, the key and most important thing is that people are willing to come together in a spirit of community. The communal aspect of Christianity is inescapable. The first two commandments are to "Love the Lord thy God" and "To Love thy neighbour as Thyself" which we are told "contain the whole of the law"[20] and as we have seen, "Love" entails an attitude of wanting what's best for someone; a willingness to give yourself for their benefit. Therefore, when we place Ricky within a Christian life and a Christian environment, not only does he aspire to have this attitude towards others but others aspire to have this attitude towards him.

For this reason alone, the issue with his working life is solved. On the one hand, he is willing to work for his boss for the very goodness that this contributes to him. On the other, his boss will seek to do everything in his power to pay his employees a fair wage because this is just in the eyes of God. This alone will have a huge effect on Ricky's motivation because not only is his boss a person worth working for from Ricky's own selfish point of view, but beyond the selfish point of view, his boss is someone worth being good to for the sake of goodness. This will extend to all of the work that Ricky does and it will extend to the people in his life who want him to excel because they – wanting what is best for Ricky – are ready and willing to allow him better opportunities.

---

20 Matthew 22:36-40

Outside of his work, Ricky is able to enjoy the wider benefits of community. Instead of coming home to a violent pair of neighbours, he finds a loving couple who are eager to give him food. Instead of being estranged from his peers outside of crime and drugs, he shares a common purpose with them to be stewards of their community, also seeking to help people in need. Again, like in the case of Carol and James, there is social pressure for people to be upright and loyal and so even when hardship strikes again when Ricky's lover betrays him, the community comes down on the side of what is right.

And so, what does Ricky's example tell us about God's intentions for the enjoyment of a Christian life?

The first thing is that he shows us that when we live by God's law, we are more likely to live lives of mutual striving and purpose (this is without even being explicit about all of the other reasons that God gives us meaning such as the striving for Heaven and the salvation of mankind!). It shows that the life that God intends for us is one full of support and good-will in which each person can find purpose in living for one-another, despite the hardships that come their way. Indeed, it would appear that in the Christian life, hardships are just another way for those who love each other to prove their love and commitment which is yet another way to strengthen the bonds between them.

Notice how small pleasures like drugs and alcohol needn't even factor into Ricky's second example; they are out-shone by everything else. By living as a Christian, his life is set on higher things which promise more fulfilment and by living in a Christian community it's far more likely that these things will be realised. Hence, we find from this example that God speaks to us through joy by saying -once again – that compared to the life of Sin, the Christian life is full of far more depth, connection and meaning. He does not intend for us to live in an atomised, meaningless malaise of malicious intent. Instead, He intends for us to live a life of meaning amongst members of a community who have their sights on things which are greater than themselves.

Consider Sarah

Sarah has just returned home from walking the dogs. Her husband greets her with a smile and hands her a cup of tea. It's autumn, her favourite time of year and the aroma of the hot drink in her hands against the slight, refreshing chill is a slice of heaven. Then she looks at her husband and feels a wave of affection for him.

They had met in medical school when she was in her mid twenties. Just before that she had travelled. Her parents had given her enough money to see the world for a couple of years. They had gifted her some money to say "well done" for all of the hard work she'd accomplished. They had always been so encouraging. That trip was the most fun she'd ever had. Yet, it made her think: was it the *happiest* she'd ever been? Surely not. What could it have been?

And then came medical school... and Mark. What struck her first was his intelligence but what really struck her was how enthusiastic he was about helping people. There was even that night where he'd put down that thug at the bar... By the time he made his proposal, it was an easy answer. He'd been loving and faithful to her ever since. And *what a father...*

The children! If it wasn't her husband, was it them who gave her the happiest moments? *Would it even be fair to count the births!?* What about when Bobby had cooked her that risotto? or when she had stayed up that night with Hannah as they did each other's hair? There was that night when they threw her that surprise for Christmas... Thinking about it almost made Sarah cry.

Then again, to be fair... there had been a few moments at work too...

Sarah loved her job. Not only did it pay well and make her a respected member of the community but it was so engaging and rewarding. Two things came to mind:

There was that day when she struggled over an old woman who had an aneurysm. The aneurysm was potentially fatal but after the surgery she held Sarah's hand and thanked her for all of the years that she would now get to spend with her grandchildren.

There was another time when she was called into emergency. Despite it not being her field of expertise, they needed her to improvise a procedure for a baby who was having trouble breathing. After that the mother couldn't even say "thank you"; she sobbed through her words too many times.

Once she took her coat off Sarah took her tea into the lounge where she and Mark sat with one of the kids as they looked over the photos from last week's holiday. She felt – and not for the first time - so happy that she could die.

As Sarah grew older she would enter her retirement. Her and Mark would use the money that they had left to travel the rest of the world. Hannah and Denny would have children of their own, all the while they would be in Sarah's company, right into her old age...

If anyone had ever asked her whether she was religious, Sarah would have hesitated. And if she was pressed, she would have said no. She had no animosity towards God or even religion; many of her friends were religious. She just didn't share the same conviction herself. It wasn't that her world-view was removed from the spiritual either. Yes, though she seldom articulated it she could sense some connection between the stars and the flowers and anytime that she beheld the Heavens or gazed into her children's eyes, she *felt* it. Maybe people would simply call it "the universe"; maybe it was explained by biology, maybe they would say it had something to do with "Karma" or the "Tao" or simply the "Way of things"... maybe some people called it Jehovah or Allah or *"God"*... it's not that she ever hated that term, it just had so much baggage and frankly, although this "bigger stuff" played a part in her life, it didn't play a central one. And that was okay. God might exist... he might not. All that Sarah knew was that when it came to "God", for here –personally- there just wasn't any *need*...

She was getting along just fine without him.

Sarah had no childhood. She would keep many of her younger memories to herself until far into her life and some she would never share with another human being until the day she died. Her parents were in the business of child trafficking and regarded their own children as just another commodity. Sarah would be put into "practice" or on "sale" from infancy, sometimes multiple times a day. By the time that she was in her teens much of the obscenity had become a matter of course. In fact, Sarah didn't know much else about life. She knew she didn't like it very much. Otherwise, she knew -according to mother- that the world was full of dangerous people who neither she nor her brothers and sisters could trust. In fact, she was always taught that they couldn't trust each-other either and this lesson had been proven to her a number of times.

She always feared mother, even more than she feared father. But he was more of a shadow in the background and didn't get too involved in the "administration". Although, when she would get older the relatively few memories she had of him would make her writhe.

At the age of 13 she had fallen into such a deep depression that she pocketed a bottle of pills that she'd been able to steal from one of her "clients" and attempted an overdose. Her brother caught her and before they knew it, mother and father had one of their "friends" on call to administer a procedure. She'd been de-detoxified and put to bed but not a day went by before her parents dragged her down to the basement, wrapped her in a blanket and beat her for her insolence. The blanket ensured that there were no bruises and so a couple of days later it was business as usual.

Sarah's life was a numb, distant heartbeat for years after that and she lived most of it somewhere in the back of her skull. Yet, she couldn't stay there forever. Some moments drew her to the surface and some were almost unendurable. One night a client paid well above the usual asking price to take her "on loan" at his home and with the request that he could be "firm". Her parents agreed so long as he promised that he would pay extra, give Sarah back and that he would pay most of the money upfront. That night he'd been far more "firm" than Sarah had expected while he'd forced her to do amphetamines, keeping her awake. However, his own concoction made him pass-out before the night was over. He'd left a window open in the back-room... Sarah's chance to escape.

She wandered the street that night in utter despair, wondering where she could go and who she could turn to. With a body full of drugs, a cold October night and not but a t-shirt and tracksuit bottoms, she understood that there was a strong chance that she could curl up in a nearby field and never need to wake up again...
She went on her way when a clear voice spoke to her, saying "It's okay. I've got you." There was no one standing near her. That voice came from somewhere even further away than the little cabin in the back of her head. Yet, it filled her. She had never felt

so comforted and never felt so much trust for anyone until she had heard that voice. With an indescribable feeling of hope, she threw herself on the mercy of the local authorities and never needed to return to her home.

Even after this, Sarah endured much. Some of the people that she formed her earlier relationships with used her damaged past to their advantage. They used her trauma and ignorance to inflict more abuse; some physical but mostly psychological. All the while, she had to deal with the after-shock of her past that could re-surface in all kinds of ways. Over time she found work and a career. Sarah learned to draw clear lines around her with a very low tolerance for anything even slightly serpentine. As a result, her circle of friends would be very small indeed but the few she had chosen had a deep quality to them. Still, she had learned to keep the world and the people in it at arms-length. On the whole, if Sarah's life had moved beyond a nightmare it persisted as a trial, forcing her to live with her scars until the very end. It wasn't that her life was an unbroken hell; indeed, there were glimpses of joy that would be as a pillar of sunlight breaking through the clouds and there would be many moments, people and places that she would appreciate. Nonetheless, the idea that she would live a "happy" life was a vacant one; a gentle sentiment for children and the ignorant which she would never mock but could never take seriously herself. No. That's not what she was here for. Yet, she did not despair of a life of misery either. And so, what was she living for?

If she was ever asked, Sarah would explain that she lived for that voice in the back of her head which she always knew and never doubted was Jesus. He had been a moment of solace for her at the brink and since then He had shone the light through the clouds onto her to show that, although she lived beneath the shade of this horrible world, there was a sun shining behind it. If it had not been for Him, not only would she have died in the shade but she would never have known that the sun existed. And so, she had not decided to chase happiness because if true happiness was anywhere, surely it would be "up there"... certainly it was not "down here". Instead, she decided to live for the person who had shown it to her. Sarah lived for Jesus. When it came down to it, it was no happy memory or fun holiday or even a loving touch which kept her going... the thing that kept her going was Him.

Commentary

If we are going to be Christians who are going to take the question of joy as seriously as possible we have to take it in its most difficult form. When we consider the role that joy plays in the Christian life and how God might speak to us through it, the examples above are comparatively "easy" compared to the example of Sarah because they provide examples of where life is largely devoid of enjoyment, yet filled by it in the Christian counterpart. However, in the case of Sarah we have one example in which life is virtually full of enjoyment without God and another in which it is practically devoid of it but with Him. The things that Christians have to contest with is this claim: that – according to Christianity – the second life is actually *better* than the first. How can this possibly be the case?

The first thing to emphasise is that if the second life is objectively better, it doesn't make it a "good" life in the sense that you would want to recommend it to anyone. The second example is horrific and at most we might say that if we ever found someone in such a situation and anything could afford them the slightest bit of solace, we would wish that for them. Better for them to never be in that situation to begin with; better to live the kind of full, happy life in the first example combined with a Love for God. Indeed, we could also point out that the second example is yet another example of a life submerged in sin. All of the suffering that Sarah experiences is due to the sin of other people and because sin is antithetical to the Will of God by its very nature, it is clear that the second example is not at all the kind of life that God intends for us. However, this isn't the issue at hand. This issue is that until now we have seen examples of how God can speak to us through joy in light of the Christian life. What are we to think now that this has been turned on its head?

The next thing to emphasise is that if we are Christians, when we consider Sarah's happy life, all of the good things in it have to be attributed to God. She just doesn't acknowledge His hand in them. It's not as if it's an example of a life *devoid* of God. To be more accurate, it is an example of a life without a recognition of the Christian God, with no clear intention to follow His Will. Doesn't that complicate the matter? After all, Sarah has achieved many good things. For example, she saved people from death as a doctor. What's more, her and her husband have remained faithful to each-other. And so it appears that she lived a life which was not only happy but *good*.

Yet... how good is good, exactly? This is the important question to consider now. As Christians we are taught that God *is* Goodness itself and being infinite, Goodness itself exceeds our comprehension of it. True Goodness is nothing short of absolute perfection. And so, what does it mean to say that Sarah lived a *good* life? Apparently, it is to say that she lived by a relatively small degree of goodness whilst not attributing it to its source. Don't get me wrong, this is not to trivialise her actions. Saving a life might be a feat far beyond what I could ever hope to achieve but by comparing it to God, we are trying to place these actions in their proper context. The crux of the issue is this: that no matter how much good Sarah lived out in her life, so long as she rejected submitting her will to Goodness Himself, she must necessarily fall short in some way. Indeed, we should say that she is only willing to pursue goodness up to a point which suits her and then go no further. Now, *how much further* could she go? How much further could any of us go if we submit our wills to God not just for now but for eternity? The point is that if she stops the buck anywhere short of God's Will, her life might be "good" but ultimately, it's not as good as it could be. And if it's not as good as it could be due to a wilful rejection of God, we have to conclude that her goodness is not really "good" because it shows a desire to fall short of perfection; the intention of the Loving God.

But then, does this not all go to show that her enjoyment of life was actually a bad thing? After all, she never felt a need to attribute anything to God and so should we say that the fact that she found life so easy kept her away from Him? Maybe. I would not be the first to argue that God speaks to us through our pain.[21] Yet, we need not go that way just yet. We can speak to the issue of joy. Pain can be a way that God speaks to us but it's not as if God needs pain to prove His existence. In the case of Sarah, God used joy to speak to her over and over again because, as we have said, all good things come from Him. In fact, all that has happened is that God has found ways to bestow a life full of gifts upon Sarah and so has not recognised where they came from.

Now, if we were to design a society to live like Sarah where everyone maximised their enjoyment without being religious we would simply create a society where everyone enjoyed the fruits of God's goodness whilst cutting it off from its source. If we are then to consider whether such a society is "good" we should return to the question: how good is good if it falls short of God?

In the examples of Ricky and Carol we had examples of how God might have spoken to them through the joys of Christian

---

21 See C.S. Lewis on *The Problem of Pain* and St Augustine's *The City of God.*

living, showing a connection to His Will and what kind of state this might put us in. In the first example of Sarah, we have the joy He permits without following His intention. Yet... one thing we could consider is: is Sarah really enjoying a life which is devoid of Christian goodness? True enough, we wouldn't say that she is living a specifically *Christian* life but she if following and enjoying many things that would be recognised as Christian virtues; the loyalty of a faithful husband... self-giving work... the recognition of beauty... again, all of these points circle back to the fact that God *is* Goodness. And so, to posit a joyful life that does not recognise Him does not present a challenge to everything else that has been said. In the cases of Carol and Ricky there was a need for this enjoyment as well as a recognition of how this need was fulfilled and according to whom. In the case of Sarah, this joy is forthcoming without recognising its source. It reminds me of a story about a Catholic Priest and a Buddhist Monk. The two are discussing the nature of religion and agree that at the heart of religion is gratitude; this affords true joy. Bemused, the priest asks the monk: "but... do you know who you are grateful to?" the monk says "No." to which the Priest replies "well... we do."[22]

All of this is to say that Sarah's life might be happy but falls short of the kind of joy experienced by Carol and Ricky in at least two respects. First, in the respect that it is limited because she is content to pursue goodness to a point and allow it to fall short. To the extent that she is not living as a Christian, she may well be lacking the real heights of joy either in this life or the life to come. In the second respect, she lacks the proper gratitude by not recognising where that joy comes from and why.

Now... what about Sarah's second example? After all of this talk about the heights of enjoyment, gratitude and the like, what are we to make of this? What has Sarah got to be grateful for?

---

22 Peter Kreeft, *40 Reasons why I'm a Catholic*

Of course, the first answer to this question would be that if Sarah lived this life of horrific suffering but was kept alive by the voice of Christ, she has that to be grateful for. But then, of course, the counter-question would be: why should Sarah be grateful to God if He allowed her to be a victim of that horrific life in the first place? This is the problem of Evil. The issue is that this work is not meant to be a theological defence of Christianity; that is to be seen elsewhere. The problem of Evil has been answered by many theologians and even in the tradition where we have the examples of people like Job or Christ Himself to consider when we are reflecting upon the role of suffering in the Christian life. The question isn't whether suffering can be a part of an *[earthly]* Christian life; every Christian knows that... instead, our question was about joy. In the examples of Ricky and Carol we saw how God could speak to His followers "through" joy by bestowing it upon the Christian life. Yet, what are we to make of Sarah's life if she finds it to be a living hell? What could He possibly be saying to her?

The first thing that comes to mind is an argument found in Augustine's *City of God*. The story goes that Augustine was being challenged by the Romans. They asked him: "tell us... if your God is Love itself... if He is *so* good and *so* just... why does He allow suffering to fall upon the just and the unjust alike?" Augustine's answer was that one reason why God allows this to happen is because by allowing the just and unjust alike to suffer, He reminds us that this world is not the one that we are made for.[23] Sarah's second example is extreme but in a fundamental way it is not unlike the examples of Ricky and Carol. Once again, Sarah finds herself in a milieu of sin. It's just that this time the sin is of such a degree that it doesn't allow for the same kind of earthly reprieve. Yet, the core lesson is the same: this is not the world that we are made for. When you or I or all of the people around us reject God's will and embrace Evil, right down to the betrayal

---

23 St Augustine's *The City of God*.

of family and abuse of innocents, they prove that they create a life which is hellish in nature. And indeed, earth is a place where that life can be made. In the positive examples of Carol and Ricky there would still have been earthly suffering; as "the just" they would have still been beset by Evil but by considering the joy that they experience in their lives it's as if God is saying to them "this is what life can be like if you follow Me." In the example of Sarah it's as if He's saying "this is what life *is* when everyone rejects me." Yet, to be clear, Sarah is the one in this example who does not reject God. She is beset by Evil because everyone else does it. Instead, she accepts God and holds onto Him as her one source of solace; as if He is a tether; a life-line to a better world beyond the one that she is suffering through.

This is the second key point, then: that joy shines through only slightly in this example, yet it is still a testament to what God intends for Her; a life lived for Him, with Him. If the only thing worth living for in this earthly life is her Saviour and His Will, what more promise is there of what this will grow into unto eternity?

Now we can see both examples for what they are but we can only see them clearly through the eyes of Heaven. Why is it that Sarah's comfortable life is *worse* than the one that she suffered through? Because in the eyes of eternity, Sarah's happy life comes up to a point, goes no further, and falls short. For the blip of enjoyment she lives through on earth she forgoes an eternity with God by neglecting a connection with Him. On the other hand, if Sarah suffers through life and the *only* thing that she holds onto is a connection with God, that connection would last into eternity and in fact, would allow her to live through something far greater than what would be enjoyed by her counterpart in the first example.

I understand full well that these conclusions might be difficult for non-Christians (they may be difficult for Christians). After all, are we really to conclude that any one of us would *prefer* the second example of Sarah's life to the first? It might appear that this is a way of waving-off the problem with the argument that "oh, it's okay because it all works out in the end". If it appears like I am trying to trivialise matters. Please understand that I am trying to do no such thing. Whether someone who had lived a life akin to Sarah's second example would go on to conclude that it was justified by God's Will is a matter unto itself which would apply to each person. Some examples do exist. Not only are there the saints who were willing to undergo untold suffering for their faith but there are victims of abuse who have since found solace in Christ. Yet, if someone lived the kind of life that has been described and found God's promise to be unjustified it would -at the very least— be understandable.

Still, dealing with these questions in full far exceeds what can be done here. Instead, the idea was to think of the place of joy or lack of joy in a Christian life... from a distance... dare we say, "coldly" in order to consider what role joy plays in our lives. From the example of Sarah, perhaps we can conclude two more things. First, that joy can be used to speak to us even if we ignore it and as Christians, we can understand that those happy people who reject God still owe their happiness to Him. Second, that even if the only "joy" or peace or solace in life is a tiny piece that God shares with us... so long as that connects us to Him, that might be a life-line to eternity and one way in which He stretches out His hand to us, across the gulf of sin, to bring us back into our Father's Arms.

Hedonism

Hedonism is evil. And there's also good reason to argue that it's the ruling ideology of the modern world. Hedonism can be understood as the idea that happiness is the meaning of life; that the best life we live is one that we enjoy as much as possible.[24] The thing is, we have been discussing the place of enjoyment in life so much in this book that this might seem like a step too far... happiness isn't *evil* is it? Isn't happiness what God wants for us? It is these kinds of questions which tell us why hedonism is so important to pull apart. In some ways, it is in communion with the Christian world-view but in other ways it is so different that it actually becomes directly opposed to it. It's worth mentioning the two main differences from the outset. First of all, the claim isn't that happiness is evil. Hedonism is the idea that happiness is the *most important* thing and this is where the danger lies. Secondly, hedonism would hold that happiness is the most important thing in life. But the question we could ask in return is: *which life?*

As we will see, these questions have an enormous impact on how hedonism is approached, what it is and how it plays out in people's lives. This chapter will consider these questions but to give it credit, it will also attempt to take hedonism in its strongest form. We might commonly imagine that hedonism is merely a shallow pursuit of simple pleasures such as money, food and sex. Yet, more sensible thinkers may well go a step further, arguing that there is a deeper, more refined form of hedonism which seeks to maximise happiness through love, brotherhood or goodwill to all mankind. While it's certainly true that this form of hedonism is more powerful than the shallow kind, it is still the case that hedonism is a problem; a deep, pervasive and *persuasive* problem that underlies the modern world that stands as a barrier against Christianity. Many who would want to

---

24 www.plato.stanford.edu/entries/hedonism/

evangelise Christianity might argue that we need to find those people who have no purpose in life and show them why that purpose is God... but these evangelists are missing something. It's not the case that non-believers have no meaning in life. As a rule, when their meaning is based on nothing transcendental it reverts to hedonism... and stays there. As such, there is more than one reason to pry it open and see what sits inside.

Pervasive?

Why can we think that Hedonism is pervasive in the modern world? The answer is quite simple... it's in any heart, mind or philosophical system that judges the value of life by the amount of enjoyment people get out of it. In its most general form, it's on the lips of any person who says that "at the end of the day... I just want to be happy." On a larger scale, we find it implied by the grand political or economic theories of the modern day. Capitalism promises the individual accumulation of wealth... but what is that wealth worth if people aren't going to enjoy it? When swathes of people enter the market with the hope of getting a better house, a better car or even a better girlfriend, they do so with the view that these things will make their lives more enjoyable. When communists argue for an equal society where people don't have to work as cogs in a meaningless, oppressive system, it appeals to people's desire for life to be better – that is to say – *more enjoyable* once the system has changed. In between, we have various arguments about the size of government, the distribution of wealth and the organising of society. On the whole, these are attempts to decide the best way to organise society so that people can, generally, enjoy their lives as much as possible. Without a secular morality which can appeal to objective morality for its own sake, this appears to be the default position.

Yet, even amongst the religious we can find a mindset which is fundamentally hedonistic. It depends what people are engaging in religion for. If someone becomes an advocate of Taoism or Buddhism because it generally seems to fit with their preferences or simply because it makes life "easier" in some way, they are a hedonist before they are a Buddhist or a Taoist. A Buddhist might find that their philosophy and practice makes them more relaxed, more accepting and more at peace with the life that they're living which makes them adhere to it. If a person forgoes their Buddhism because it doesn't make their life more pleasant as a whole, we would say that their main priority is their enjoyment and that they will give up their Buddhism when it no longer serves this. This can apply to Christians too. Many avowed Christians might attend Church because it's full of friendly people; because it's a place to dance or sing; because it's a place to see friends and provides a feeling that they're part of a larger community serving a larger purpose... in brief, because it makes their life more pleasant. Are these things trivial? No. But they are secondary to the *Truth* of Christianity as-such. If such a Christian were to forego their faith because it made their life unduly difficult, it would prove that their enjoyment was in fact their priority and that their Christianity was simply a means to this end. In fact, they would be Christians in name alone.

Hence, to the extent that we see this idolising of enjoyment, whether it be explicitly or under the guise of other ideals, we can say that hedonism pervades modern society.

Persuasive?

Hedonism is persuasive because pleasure feels good. The philosophies that reject hedonism are those that demand that we live for things beyond pleasure, regardless of how we feel about it. Yet, it's common-sense to recognise that people tend to have an aversion to what feels bad and are drawn to what feels good. There are exceptions to this but they are grounded in transcendent ideals. Unless those are assumed, hedonism is persuasive because it constantly coaxes people to follow their desires. To the extent that there isn't a recognised standard which transcends happiness which is imposed on the individual either by themselves or by society, the individual inclination is to listen to one's desires and move towards them. If objective morality is like a magnet that pulls people upwards towards a set standard, hedonism is like gravity; the force that pulls everyone back down to their desires once the moral magnetism fades away.

Deep and Shallow

If we're going to contend with hedonism properly, we have to contend with it in its strongest form. We have to recognise that it comes in two kinds. To begin with, there are those who argue that our lives are most enjoyable when we chase the things that we commonly recognise as pleasurable. The cartoon version of a hedonist is a drug-taking, jet-setting millionaire playboy who spends his time eating five-star meals and having sex with hundreds of beautiful women. This is the "shallow" hedonist (as we might call it). This has largely been dealt with in the chapters above. We saw how both Ricky and particularly Carol found a diminishing return in their shallow pleasures. Yet, if you want some real-world examples you can look to the scores of celebrities who have lived hollow lives, despite their levels of money and fame.[25]

Instead, we find that people recommend other ways to be happy. Instead of focusing on money, power or fame, the recommendation is to focus on things like peace, compassion and the relationships that we form with other people. This is what we

---

25 https://www.therichest.com/expensive-lifestyle/12-rich-successful-people-who-were-miserable/
https://www.therichest.com/entertainment/15-celebs-who-prove-money-cant-buy-happiness/
https://www.oddee.com/item_98693.aspx

could call a kind of "deep" hedonism. The focus is still on being as happy as possible but the enjoyment isn't to be found in "pleasure" as-such but in the higher things of life. This is the kind of hedonism that we would see in the Christian who goes to Church because of how it serves his life. We could think of it in these terms: that Christianity is being "sold"[26] to him on the grounds that the meaning and community that it will give him will maximise his sense of enjoyment or fulfilment more than the alternatives. He might accuse the playboy of being a hedonist but in fact this man is simply being more intelligent about his hedonism. He could approach it with the attitude that "I want to be more happy" but instead of aiming for the happiness directly (which will actually make it harder to attain), he aims for other things such as love and community, understanding that the happiness that he achieves as a by-product of these things will actually be greater than the sum of happiness he gets by pursuing happiness itself.[27] Now, such a man need not hold any of these ideas explicitly. Instead, this is a case of drawing-out the logic that such an approach to life can be based upon.

Deep hedonism is in an altogether different class from "shallow" hedonism because it appears to incorporate every important and positive element into life. Deep hedonism gives man a reason to be loving, kind, co-operative, compassionate and to form strong communities. You see, hedonism in and-of-itself doesn't need to lead to hollow, selfish, destructive nihilism. Given the rationale of an intelligent "deep" hedonist you may well be able to form a society which is both stable and mutually-supportive. Even with the pursuit of happiness underlying it,

---

26 Even if this man is the one making the "sale" to himself.

27 For a full treatment of these claims, read *The Happiness Hypothesis* by Jonathan Haidt. Haidt's work speaks directly to the idea of "deep" hedonism. He gives all of the reasons for why – if you want to be happy – you really shouldn't aim for happiness itself and you should seek other things instead. He also uses the relevant psychological literature to show why the pursuit of things like money or pleasure are dead-ends.

deep hedonism can be at once meaningful and moral. It is an approach to hedonism which says "we should all be happy, but all of us will be happier if we're good."

This is the form of hedonism we need to address. It's too easy and too dismissive to attack shallow hedonism. Instead, if anything is more likely to offer itself as an alternative to Christian morality in the minds of modern men it is this idea which makes morality and stable society the handmaiden of the self-interested drive for happiness.

Hedonism is Evil

And so, what's the problem? The problem is that hedonism by any other name is still hedonism. Even if we recognise that there is a more nuanced, more advanced and dare we say more "noble" type of hedonism which encourages the fellowship of man, the problem remains that the goal is placed on the enjoyment of life and all else becomes secondary to this. In fairness, someone like Jonathan Haidt would point out that his advice is precisely that we should *not* make happiness our highest goal but prioritise other things *if* we want to be as happy as possible... to which we could retort: "yes... *if* you want to be as happy as possible. You're still selling these other goals as if happiness is the thing that the person is trying to pursue."

This is the first major problem for hedonism. It destroys itself.[28] We see this very clearly with shallow hedonism in which the process of chasing pleasure for its own sake makes people more miserable. Yet, it also applies to deep hedonism. Three contingencies are at play... if we define happiness as "maximal enjoyment":

---

28 Again, see *The Happiness Hypothesis* by Jonathan Haidt

1. *If* happiness is aimed at for its own sake, happiness gets diminished and so hedonism dissolves itself.

2. *If* other things are prioritised over happiness in order to increase happiness, happiness is still in fact the main goal, which leads us back to the same problem.

3. *If* happiness is genuinely discounted as the second goal and someone embraces something else as their highest goal, even if we were to argue that such a person experiences a maximum amount of happiness he is in fact no longer a hedonist.

Basically, either you can be a hedonist and the pursuit of happiness diminishes itself or you can just not be a hedonist.

That's the first issue: the inherent inconsistency with the ideal itself. But what makes it *evil*?

Hedonism is evil because if you pursue happiness for its own sake and not morality for its own sake, it follows that you should bend morality in order to serve your happiness. To begin with, we could never explain the morality of heroic sacrifices. If happiness is the most important thing in life, why would you ever give up your life for anything? After all, your life is the very thing that contains all possibility of enjoyment. If everyone were a hedonist, it would simply make no sense for anyone to give up their lives for anyone or anything else. This feeds into another aspect of why hedonism is evil...

Hedonism is evil because evil can by threatening to take your happiness away or even your life. Let's say that your government is becoming psychopathically tyrannical. If you are a hedonist you will only stand against that government if you feel sure that you will have a net gain of enjoyment as a result and that you won't die during your resistance. If either of these happen, resistance makes no sense. A tyrant could encroach on your life more and more; strip away one freedom after another... threaten your job your home and your children... but up until the point that they put a gun to your head, they still have something to leverage: your comfort. Even if a tyrannical government made your life miserable compared to the life you lived when your country was free, you might still have some small level of comfort left. And if you are a hedonist, that small level of comfort means everything to you. Let's say that evil starts by taking away your freedom to travel... you should resist but you won't because you can still go to bars and restaurants... then these are taken away... you should resist but you won't because you still have your TV... Hence, evil is allowed to encroach upon you because if you're a hedonist, at the end of the day, ideals like justice, morality, truth and freedom are just secondary means to an end. If the fight to uphold any of these entails a life which is less enjoyable than one in which you allow things to slide... well then, no reason to fight. And evil can have its way... a deep hedonist would argue that it is actually much more fulfilling to live a life in which you stand up for justice and fight for the good but such an argument only goes so far. Living a life in favour of the good only makes sense up to the point where you can carry on enjoying yourself. Would a hedonist uphold the good if that required them to embrace abject pain or even death? Of course not.

This speaks to yet another reason why hedonism is evil. It makes morality a matter of convenience for individuals. If the pursuit of happiness can overlap with morality, great. But if not, then what? Otherwise, why not mix-and-match? Why not choose a set of morals that appear to be the most pleasing to you; that will allow you to enjoy life the most? What's more, why not do that with truth? We could go a step further and suggest that hedonism is one of the underlying motivators of modern relativism. Objective truth is a constraint by its very nature and determines that things are true and false, right and wrong regardless of our preference. Those who believe in objective truth, be they religious or not, recognise an order of reality that we must bend to whether we enjoy it or not. A hedonist on the other hand can wear their beliefs like different outfits. If happiness is the main thing, why not consider yourself a Christian one day and a Muslim the next depending on how each religion makes you feel in the moment? That these belief systems recognise themselves to be objective is besides the point. The objective value of truth is secondary to enjoyment. Hence, hedonism gives a rationale for corrosion; not only of morality but truth as a whole. Therefore, we have another reason for why hedonism is evil.

Finally, hedonism is evil because it justifies any selfish desire. It is the morality of pride. From the point of view of the one who wants to be happy, that is the most important thing and any concerns for an obligation that creates a binding concern for others is simply an economic way for them to remain happy. They expect to live under the "idea" of morality so that other people feel bad for doing harm to them, which makes their life better and so they are content to play along. However, a genuine hedonist would see no problem with committing and enjoying evil if they could get away with it. Why would they? After all, happiness; individual happiness... *their* happiness is the most important thing in life. If *anything* threatened that the frank, consistent, logical thing to do would be to step-over or even destroy that barrier. Such a barrier could be any moral system or concern which regards the individual's enjoyment as secondary to goodness itself. Hence, evil can be expedient. If someone genuinely enjoys torturing children and they can get away with it, there's nothing really *wrong* with what they are doing if you're a hedonist. You can say that it's unpleasant for you... you can say that it's unpleasant for the child... you can say that it's not "useful" for society... but at the end of the day, there's nothing really wrong with it. He's playing by the same rules as you are. At the end of the day, he just wants to be happy too.

Which Life?

Perhaps we can try and give hedonism as much credit as possible. Perhaps we can argue that there are people who live and fight for morality even unto death. These would be the kind of people who would say "I would rather die than have let them be evil because if I continued to live in a world where I didn't fight, my life wouldn't be worth living." A hedonist may well use this line of reasoning to justify deeply moral decisions which are still made in the service of one's enjoyment, even if the person being moral isn't thinking about it in those terms.

The most pertinent example of this that I've come across is in the work of Vicktor Frankyl[29]. A survivor of the Nazi concentration camps, he recounts a story of how there would be some prisoners who gave up their ration of bread to people they felt were in greater need than themselves. The bread ration was so pitiful that giving it away was tantamount to giving away their life. The crux of the matter is this: that these men were willing to suffer and die for others, some of whom were strangers. How would a hedonist explain this? A hedonist might explain it this way: they could say that despite how painful it was to give away their bread, there must have been some part of their conscience that was motivating them the other way. Yes, they might feel *physically* worse but they might have derived deep *emotional* satisfaction from doing what they felt was right. They were willing to die because they would rather experience satisfaction for a few days than live without it for a few more weeks. It was actually the more enjoyable way for them to live.

Even if we were to take this line of thinking, two things recur again:

---

29 Vicktor Frankyl, *Man's Search for Meaning*

1. The men making this sacrifice did not prioritise their own enjoyment, even if we say that they gained some as a result of being good, and

2. To understand this kind of action, we have to understand what kind of satisfaction can be so deep that someone is willing to give up their life, which *includes the possibility of all future satisfaction.*

You see, it's one thing to argue about prisoners making the most of their last days with no other prospect of living but we also need to consider the rationale of people who could have continued to live for years after their chance to sacrifice arose, yet chose to sacrifice their lives anyway.

One *could* argue that people are still serving enjoyment or "happiness" but at the very least, we would have to re-consider our definition of happiness if we are to make it fit into this paradigm. You see, we have been discussing the benefits of enjoyment throughout this book, recognising that a state of bliss is at once something that God intends for us and something that we can get glimpses of in this life. Happiness appears to have its place within the divine plan. Yet, hedonism is evil. Perhaps this is a good place to emphasise that hedonism has been regarded as the attitude that the most important thing we can do is maximise happiness in *this life*.

If we assume the existence of Heaven, many of the things that make hedonism evil no longer apply. If Heaven exists, evil can no longer hold our happiness to ransom because we will believe that the happiness it would try to hold against us does not belong to this world and the powers that rule it but instead, belongs to God almighty and in the life to come. If Heaven exists, martyring yourself for a righteous cause makes sense because you are simply exchanging the limited happiness of this life for the eternal happiness to come...

Does this mean that a good Christian is just a very clever hedonist? No. And this is where we have to be *very* careful about the nuance of the argument.

Happiness is a consequence; a reward; a by-product of a perfect Christian life. But in the sense that hedonism makes happiness the *purpose* of life, perfect Christianity is not hedonistic. The first two commandments are not to "be happy" but to "Love God" and "Love thy neighbour as thyself". The Christian commandments call us to look *outwards;* to interests and values beyond the bounds of our self-interest. Hedonism, ultimately, remains selfish. At its core it is about how enjoyable *my* life is, making this the cosmic measure of value. Christianity denounces this attitude and to its credit, so does a version of deep hedonism but as we have seen... this kind of hedonism turns out to not be hedonism at all.

Yet, the point wasn't to make hedonism compatible with the Christian paradigm. The point to make was that a deep hedonist would still need to appeal to something beyond this life in order to take their argument as far as it can go. As Christians, we can lay hedonism to one side but even when we are encountered by hedonists with noble intentions who try to sell self-sacrifice on the grounds of enjoyment we can point out to them that they would have to at least posit the idea of a positive afterlife for that idea to make sense.

In sum, hedonism and even deep hedonism always fall short. In its common form, hedonism is a glutton that eats his own hands because the hunger for pleasure grows the more that it is consumed. This approach to life is evil because it's shallow and selfish. It leads us to place secondary things first, to forgo things of lasting beauty and would even lead us to bend morality to our own comfort. Then again, a deep hedonist could over-come many of these objections. They would argue that if we are to find the best forms of happiness in this life we shouldn't live in the shallow pursuit of pleasure; we *should* try to be selfless and moral and we should uphold truth and beauty as if they do exceed our own preferences. Hence, to be as happy as possible we have to stop caring about being happy. Thus, alas, this approach falls short too. Either it is made with the appeal to the selfish pursuit of happiness in which case it entails all of the core problems of hedonism, or it is made with the argument that we should forego the pursuit of happiness as our goal, in which case hedonism disproves itself in order to make itself work.

We might call elements of Christianity hedonistic because they do concern the attainment of happiness but Christianity isn't hedonism because the selfish pursuit of happiness isn't the Christian's goal.[30] This is why hedonism – even deep hedonism – is evil. Deep hedonism holds the promise of happiness with all the trimmings including meaning, community, morality and a sense of the divine. In brief, it's another way of offering all of the things that Christianity offers without the Christianity. But here's the rub... if Christianity is true, these things can only be truly realised through Christianity and not under the guise of something else. As a result, such a philosophy becomes another distraction; just another alternative to giving our lives to God. Therefore, if shallow hedonism is a bare-faced fraud, deep hedonism is an imposter, dressed in the garb of truth with the same promises on its lips... unable to keep its word.

To really seal an iron lid on this point, we could say one more thing.

The devil likes hedonism. If he could sell it to the world, he would (in fact, I believe that's exactly what he's trying to do). In its shallow form, hedonism distracts people from God and throws them directly into the arms of sin. Every time a man fornicates or exhibits greed or gorges himself like a glutton in the pursuit of

---

30 What are we to make of the passages in the Bible where Jesus promises eternal joy? Does He mention Heaven as if it's the whole point? Not exactly. More will be said on this in due course.

pleasure as they try to fill the God-shaped chasm in their soul... the devil smiles. As for the deep form... every time a man tries to surgically remove justice, hope, love, charity, community and peace from their source... every time a man exhausts his own happiness and tries to build a happy world without God... the devil smiles the wider... and starts to laugh.

Christian Happiness

We shouldn't make happiness life's highest goal. To do so would be to make us hedonists, and this is evil. Yet, the Christian life is not devoid of happiness. And so, what place, exactly, does happiness hold in the Christian life?

Happiness or joy?

What *is* happiness? We have been using this word in a number of ways throughout this book to explore a number of different things. It has a broad use in the English vocabulary and so we can use it in a broad way to understand it from many different angles. Yet, if we want to hone-in on what happiness really is in the Christian life we should try to get a clear understanding of what the word means. What's more important is to understand the term "joy". Until now, "happiness", "pleasure", "joy", "enjoyment," have seen their meanings blended, much as we blend them in day-to-day life. However, drawing happiness apart from joy could be particularly useful because in the Bible, God appeals to our joy far more often than He appeals to our happiness.

And so, let's return to our question: what is happiness?

According to the Oxford English Dictionary, Happiness is:

1. *the state of feeling or showing pleasure*

2. *the state of being satisfied that something is good or right*[31]

This is the definition that we've been using so far. Happiness is a state of positive feeling or satisfaction and we've

---

31 https://www.oxfordlearnersdictionaries.com/definition/english/happiness?q=happiness

been able to place our common-use ideas of "pleasure" and "enjoyment" under this heading too.

Now, for some, the concept goes a bit deeper. For example, the philosopher Aristotle argued that happiness was our highest goal in life but the word he used for this was *Eudaimonia*. However, this happiness does *not* entail a state of positive mind or feeling. Instead, *Eudaimonia* is simply the state of attaining our highest good.[32] "Feeling good" might come along with this, but not necessarily.

St. Thomas Aquinas, on the other hand, uses the term *Beatitudo* when he speaks of happiness and this term denotes happiness with further connotations of blessedness.[33] Hence, this word already has a divine element woven into its makeup.

Finally, there is the Bible's use of "happiness" which is usually the ancient Greek term *Makarios*[34]. This term is more often translated to "blessed" and in fact "happiness" and "blessed" are often inter-changeable under this definition.[35] Hence, the New-Testament use of "happiness" does not so much emphasise a state of positive feeling but good fortune and divine favour. Once again, positive feeling might be entailed by this but not necessarily (for example, people aren't placed in a state of profound pleasure simply once they are blessed).

Therefore, in all of these examples we see definitions of happiness which entail more than states of pleasure or positive feeling. These definitions of happiness consistently speak to something higher such as the Good and The Divine. Hence, when we are thinking about being "happy" Christians, it should go

---

32 https://www.britannica.com/topic/eudaimonia
33 https://latin-dictionary.net/definition/6247/beatitudo-beatitudinis,
    https://www.wordsense.eu/beatitudo/,
    https://dictionary.university/beatitudo
34 As seen in John 13:12-17 or Revelation 1:3
35 https://www.bibletools.org/index.cfm/fuseaction/Lexicon.show/ID/
    G3107/makarios.htm

without saying that we are already weaving these things into our aspirations.

What about joy?

According to the Oxford English Dictionary, the word "joy" simple means:

1. *a feeling of great happiness*[36]

And so that doesn't tell us much. We would conclude that joy just means "very happy".

However, joy is used a lot in the Bible and has a distinctive meaning. In the ancient Greek the word use for "joy" is *Chara*[37]. This word does denote those "happy" qualities of being "cheerful" and "glad" but it also denotes the *reception* of these things or the *cause for occasion* of them.[38] If this term is relating to happiness, it's as if its not only relating to the happiness itself but to its source and foundation which gives it the distinctively *joyous* quality. Indeed, what's even more interesting is that one analysis of the ancient Greek treats the word for "joy" as a cognate with the word for "Grace". Two words are cognates when they share the same etymological source and so we could say that the words for "joy" and "Grace" are closely, genetically related in the ancient Greek.[39] Hence, there is strong reason to think that "joy" and "Grace" are speaking to the same thing. Grace, after all, denotes a gift, a blessing or a kindness[40]. This means that we have a very close connection between true happiness in the form of joy and its source. We are also given the idea that the same word that

---

36 https://www.oxfordlearnersdictionaries.com/definition/english/joy?q=joy
37 As found in John 16:22 or Romans 14:17
38 https://www.bibletools.org/index.cfm/fuseaction/Lexicon.show/ID/ G5479/chara.htm
39 https://biblehub.com/greek/5479.htm
40 https://biblehub.com/greek/5485.htm

would point us towards the source of happiness which transforms it into joy is Grace.

This tells us at least two things. First of all, it tells us that if joy is the higher form of happiness that we seek, the highest form of happiness depends on its source and as Christians, of course, it is plain to see that this source of joy which so gives it is elevated nature is no other than God. The Second thing it tells us is that there is this connection between joy and a gift, a blessing or a kindness... are we to say that joy relates not only to the receiver but the manner in which is received? Is it too much of a reach to say that we are talking about *Love*? It is interesting to see how these deep themes surrounding happiness – *true* happiness – keep circling back onto the same idea.

Love

And so, what *is* Love? This is a question which is fundamental to Christian joy and indeed to all of Christian living. It speaks directly to the heart of who we are, what we are here for and Who made us.

First, we can start with the dictionary definition. According to the Oxford English Dictionary, love is defined as:

1. *a very strong feeling of liking and caring for somebody/something, especially a member of your family or a friend*

2. *a strong feeling of romantic attraction for somebody*

3. *the strong feeling of pleasure that something gives you*

4. *a person, a thing or an activity that you like very much*[41]

This forth definition captures the general usage the most concisely; we tend to say we "love" something when we like it a

---

41 https://www.oxfordlearnersdictionaries.com/definition/english/love_1?q=love

lot. Then again, the nuanced layers of meaning become very relevant when we are trying to express this idea. After all, we use the same word, "love" when we say that we "love" our children and we "love" a slice of cake. Yet, the quality of this "love" is so different that it almost seems blasphemous to say that we are referring to the same thing in both cases. We see this in the definitions when we see how the attribution of the word can change from one use to the next (a strong feeling of *attraction* for a lover, or a strong feeling of *affection* for a family member). Yet, we can take this further...

Simply put, the English understanding of the word "love" is too limited. Instead, we should turn to the ancient Greeks who distinguish between four types of love.[42] The four words that the Greeks used for "love" are *Stroge, Eros, Philios* and *Agape*[43].

Stroge is affectionate or habitual love that you might have for a neighbour or a cat.

Eros is erotic or romantic love, the kind that you feel for a wife and the kind that we would use when we talk about "falling in love".

Philios is "brotherly" love or the love between friends; typically created in the connection that two people feel when they know that they are aiming their lives towards the same end.

Agape is divine love. It is the love the pours out onto the beloved simply because the one who Loves intends what is best for the one who is loved. In fact, we would say that the core principle of *Agape* is this: that one has *Agape* when their intentions are filled with what is best for the other person, without regard for their own selfish interest. The closest analogue we have to this in human life is in the love felt by a parent for a child.

---

42 Amongst other places, these are explained in *The Four Loves* by C.S. Lewis.

43 Pronounced "ah-gah-pay"

The four loves are not exclusive. We can experience combinations of all four in many different ways but we won't concern ourselves with all four kinds of Love now. Of course, the one kind of Love which concerns us the most is this last one: *Agape*; Divine Love...

This is Christian Love. We are told by St. Paul that "God demonstrates his own *Agape* for us in this: whilst we were still sinners, Christ died for us.[44] We are told by St. John that "Whoever does not love does not know God, because God is *Agape*."[45] And we are told by Christ Himself what contains the whole of the law: "*Agape* the Lord your God with all your heart and with all your soul and with all your mind and with all your strength. And *Agape* your neighbour as yourself. There is no commandment greater than these."[46]

Love is the most important thing in life. It is our highest calling; our highest command and the very nature of our Divine Creator. What's more, it seems like no mistake that the Christian conception of joy would appear to be so closely related to Love. In fact, it must be entailed by it. If Christ makes Love our highest commandment yet tells us that we will find *joy* by pleasing Him, it follows that Love is the means to our joy. Yet, we come back to a point that we have seen again and again: that Love is *not* concerned with one's self. Love is concerned with another. Love is concerned with what is best for someone regardless of what our own preferences might be telling us. Hence, we can attain joy through love but not if our concern for joy is the main thing.

---

44   Romans, 5:8
45   1 John 4:8
46   Mark 12:29-31

Words of Wisdom

"May the God of hope fill you with all joy and peace in believing, so that by the power of the Holy Spirit you may abound in hope" (Romans 15:13).

"Man cannot live without joy. That is why one deprived of spiritual joys goes over to carnal pleasures." - Saint Aquinas

"No man truly has joy unless he lives in love." - Saint Aquinas

"God alone can satisfy the will of man, according to the words of the Psalms (102:5): "Who alone satisfies your desire with good things." Therefore, God alone constitutes man's happiness." - Saint Aquinas

"For the kingdom of God is not a matter of eating and drinking, but of righteousness, peace and joy in the Holy Spirit..." (Romans 14: 17)

"The most venerable, clearly understood, enlightened, and reliable constant in the world is not only that we want to be happy, but that we want only to be so. Our very nature requires it of us." - Saint Augustine

"When large numbers of people share their joy in common, the happiness of each is greater because each adds fuel to the other's flame." - Saint Augustine

"Delight yourself in the Lord, and he will give you the desires of your heart" (Psalm 37:4).

"There is a joy which is not given to the ungodly, but to those who love Thee for Thine own sake, whose joy Thou Thyself

art. And this is the happy life, to rejoice to Thee, of Thee, for Thee; this it is, and there is no other." - Saint Augustine

"*I have told you this so that my joy may be in you and that your joy may be complete.*" (John 15:11)

What does happiness mean to Christians? What role does it play in the Christian life? We have been exploring this throughout the course of this book but now it is time to try and hone-in on the answer.

A good place to start is by considering the statements above found in the Bible and made by two men who were arguably the two greatest Catholic philosophers to have ever lived. At this juncture, we have much to learn by doing two things. First, we can compare these statements to each-other and try to discover what they can tell us about the Christian approach. Second, we can compare what these statements tell us with what we have discussed throughout this book. On the surface, it appears as if some of these claims should make us re-consider our approach to happiness. Instead, perhaps they allow us to see it more completely. We won't try to compare all of the statements with each-other but let's take a look at some of the key ones and see what they can tell us...

"Man cannot live without joy. That is why one deprived of spiritual joys goes over to carnal pleasures." - Saint Aquinas

"For the kingdom of God is not a matter of eating and drinking, but of righteousness, peace and joy in the Holy Spirit..." (Romans 14: 17)

"Delight yourself in the Lord, and he will give you the desires of your heart" (Psalm 37:4).

"May the God of hope fill you with all joy and peace in believing, so that by the power of the Holy Spirit you may abound in hope" (Romans 15:13).

These passages appear to tell us two things. Firstly, they echo the thoughts that have already been sharing about shallow hedonism. In fact, this is explicit when Aquinas says that we will be given over to "Carnal pleasures". The lack of true joy leaves a hole. Men so often try to fill that hole with sex, drugs, money and power... but they never will. Our joy is to be found in things of a deeper nature. Then the next passage tells us exactly where we will find this... that it is in the Lord that we will realise the desires of our hearts.

The second thing they speak to is how joy sustains us. "No man can live without joy" says Aquinas, and St. Paul wrote of joy as a way to fill us with hope. Hence, the picture is like this: imagine a group of men who are trying to look for the setting sun. The sun does not intend to rise again but has hidden itself behind the horizon leaving the men in a world which is cold and dark.[47] Yet, the last rays of the sun can still be seen flickering in the distance, growing more vivid with each passing step. Not only this, but the sun has left traces of itself on the earth. The men are able to light fires on their journey; smaller versions of that great

---

47 If we were to be strict in our analogy, we would point out that the men were the ones who caused the sun to set in the first place...

fire which they seek which is the end of their journey. These fires keep the men warm; they are islands of ease through a long journey of struggle and indeed, without these flames... no man can live.

The analogy is imperfect but it is as if joy is granted to us like campfires on a journey. We have hope that we will find the source of joy one day and indeed, we have evidence of the light it shines, even if it is not present here on this earth. Still, in the meantime, the joy that we are given is imperfect but it sustains us on our journey; it keeps us warm, it keeps us alive and it gives us hope. And so, perhaps this is one way that we can understand joy in the Christian journey: it is a campfire for our long journey. Yet, woe to the man who mistakes the campfire for the journey itself and who stops on the dark road before he has seen the sun.

"When large numbers of people share their joy in common, the happiness of each is greater because each adds fuel to the other's flame." - Saint Augustine

"No man truly has joy unless he lives in love." - Saint Aquinas

Now we are starting to get a deeper picture of what joy entails. It entails Love and as we have seen, God *is* Love.[48] He is a light that shines unto all of us and we are to shine that light forth in turn. When we do so, we will find that our own joy will shine all the brighter. Thus, Love is found in joy. God is our Heavenly *Father*. The joy of a child isn't something that a parent selfishly consumes for themselves. Instead, the joy is something reflected by the parent. They love and care for their child so much that the

---

48 1 John 4:16

joy of the child is felt as if it is their own. Yet, it is not because they are trying to make the child a slave to their happiness. It is because the parent loves the child first and the joy follows. By emphasising Love above joy we are called to treat everyone in this manner; to understand that Love and joy are things which are gained when they are shared. Therefore, we find that joy isn't attained within ourself or with reference to ourselves. Love is something that's facing outwards. Hence, love is something to be found when we are looking outwards and do away with the concern for our own gratification.

Not only are we given joy as a respite from the dark human life but we are given that flame to warm others. When those flames are kept apart, the world turns cold.

"There is a joy which is not given to the ungodly, but to those who love Thee for Thine own sake, whose joy Thou Thyself art. And this is the happy life, to rejoice to Thee, of Thee, for Thee; this it is, and there is no other." - Saint Augustine

"I have told you this so that my joy may be in you and that your joy may be complete." (John 15:11)

Finally, we have the passages that tell us what we really need to look at. We saw above how joy is found through Love and how Love looks beyond itself. Well, ultimately, what Love looks to is God. God, being the greatest thing beyond ourselves, He is the greatest thing that we can give Love to. In fact, God is the source of all Love and so He is the greatest place for us to draw Love from and reflect Love back to. Yet, we are not told to do this for the sake of joy but "for thine own sake". We are not to Love God in pursuit of our own interest but for His and because God is

Love, this interest in Him spills-over onto everyone else. We are to seek the Good of everyone and everything for its own sake. This is the source of eternal joy.

We see this in the words of Christ in The Gospel of St. John. Being God, He shows His interest in sharing His joy; in letting His Love spill-over; because "my joy may be in you". This is the example He sets. He seeks to make other people joyful. This is His Love. Being the Heavenly father, He wants what is best for His children. Perhaps those who are parents or siblings are best poised to understand this. A son loves his mother and asks her: what can I do to help you? And the mother answers: "just look after your little sister." When the son's love is directed up to his parent or to the side for his sibling, the answer ends up being the same. "Love one another; as I have loved you."[49]

Before we continue, I'd like to share a final thought about the nature of joy. C.S. Lewis once made a claim about how Love is the thing that allows us to understand God's Divine nature as a trinity (or how the trinity allows us to understand that God is Love). His point was that if we are to accept from scripture that God is Love, this is hard to make sense of because Love has an object which is beyond the self. In essence, how can God *be* Love unless He has someone *to* Love other than Himself? The answer is that God is more than one person by His very nature.[50] Hence, His Love is never actually selfish, even if it's for Himself (or we should strictly say for one of the three people who constitute Himself). God is like a family with three members: all perfectly good, all perfectly Loving and all three so perfectly rejoicing in the Goodness and Love of the other that their joy is eternal. Never being truly selfish, God's Love is always being reflected. Like Augustine's flames, the fire of Love is always being lighted anew by being passed from one hand to the next. When God was

---

49   John 15:12
50   *Mere Christianity* by C.S. Lewis

the only being that existed, that flame was being passed between the three members of the Trinity. Now that God has created, He calls upon all beings who have the choice to do so to pass that fire onto everyone else and, in turn, to pass it back to Him.

Now we can compare our conclusion with the discussion that we had in the preceding chapters.

What is the role of happiness in the Christian life?

The first thing that we can conclude is that it's not the priority. When we make happiness the priority, we lead to hedonism which dissolves happiness itself, as well as our moral purpose. We can use happiness in the broader sense to encompass joy but even then, it should not be our highest goal. Even when we are told by someone like St. Aquinas that no man can live without joy, we find that joy does not take the place of highest priority.

Instead, we find that joy is superseded by our deepest moral purpose: Love. Without Love, we are lacking in joy. Hence, if man cannot live without joy, the fullness of life is found through joy and the fullness of joy is found through Love. Thus, it is Love that fills our purpose. Yet, he who loves does not regard himself. He is willing to sacrifice himself for the better of others. He does not look to his own joy but theirs. He does not look to his own *life,* but theirs. By recognising this, perhaps we are better able to understand Christ's claim that "whoever wants to save their life will lose it, but whoever loses their life for me will find it."[51] God is Love. Christ is Love. Hence, whoever is willing to give their life for Love will find the fullness of their life realised in the Love that

---

51 Matthew 16:25

they were willing to give, and by receiving the joy and Love of Christ.

When we compare this to all else that has been said above we realise that the question of "enjoying" the Christian life is secondary. We began by discussing how God can speak to us through joy and so, what are we to make of this? We can now conclude that joy speaks to us by saying that Love is the source of joy. When we considered Carol, Ricky or even Sarah we saw how they partook in joy when they were putting their efforts into things that were beyond themselves. They were trying to live lives in service to God and as a result were trying to Love Him and one-another.

Yet, these examples were also cartoons of the perfect Christian life. If we were all able to live it, surely we would share joy more abundantly. Alas, we live in a cold world of sin and this kind of life is rare. Even when we try our best to do good, we are beset with the evil around us. Even then, God appears to kindle joy like a flame in the night. Maybe He gives us just enough to be a beacon unto Heaven so that we are motivated to seek Him further, knowing full well that one thing we have to forego on that journey towards Him is the very concern for our own happiness that motivated us in the first place.

There's plenty more to say (there always is) but as of now, it seems like all of the most important things that needed to be said have been. We've considered the role of enjoyment in numerous ways; by considering the Christian life, by considering how people live it out, by considering the *lack* of joy in a Christian life and by comparing it to the various shades of hedonism. After all, perhaps we can say this: enjoying life has its place. If God did not intend for us to enjoy anything, we would presume that Heaven is merely cold. Yet, enjoyment is not the end. Especially not for this life. We were made to find joy but we were made – foremost- to find Love. Only in the second will we find the first. Enjoyment is a companion; a compliment given to the Christian life, but it is not its core. We should appreciate whatever enjoyment we have the fortune to experience without presumption and we should look forward to what waits in the life to come. Yet, all the while, whether we are enjoying ourselves or not, we should always be focused on doing what is right.

Doing Good unto Others

Every good thing we do must pertain to Love.

This is not a soft sentiment but an ironclad truth which follows from everything that has been said so far. Love is man's highest Good, leading Him to His Creator. Love entails doing and intending what is best for someone else. What is best for someone else is also Love. That is to say, if Love were a "thing" it is the best thing that James can possess. However, James only really "has" it if he gives it to John (and God). John only really "has" it if he gives it to Peter, and so on...

If this is the case, what does it mean for us to do good unto others?

Let's approach this in a different way...

Praying for a man's soul is an act of Love because there can be nothing better for him than the attainment of his salvation.

Yet, why do we also regard it as an act of Love to heal a friend when they are sick or to carry their load when they are weary? These are the painful burdens of life but simply suffering pain in life isn't necessarily *bad,* especially if this can motivate us to seek the Good. What I'm trying to say is... can we call the earthy goods that we do for one-another "good"? After all, they are of the earth and not of Heaven...

I think the answer is this: when we effect someone's earthly life, even when this has no clear reference to Heaven, it can still be an act of Love because we can lead people *through* earth unto Heaven.

What do I mean by this...?

I mean that when you give a needy stranger a warm meal, the sustenance and flavour of the meal are secondary – or perhaps – *accidental* to something greater. The man feels pain. You give him the meal and take the pain away. What's more, you tell him that what's mine is yours; that you are willing to sacrifice part of your wordly existence to his. Hence, you are showing the man Love. You are showing him that another gives themselves to him and that this can give him reprieve. We could say it's a microcosm of joy which works for the same reason. Aside from the warmth of the meal, the *act* has a warmth of its own which speaks to the Divine. Knowing that act doesn't only teach the man that Love is present but it might inspire him to embrace that Love in his own life. Hence, even when we try to show Love through the earthly comforts of unbelievers maybe we are throwing sparks onto the kindling of their soul... using our own Love to set theirs aflame.

Yet, let us not conclude that Love is all soft soap. We should always keep in mind that God is Love Himself, yet wiped Sodom and Gomorrah from the face of the earth.[52] Jesus meek and mild was not beyond lashing blasphemers in the House of His father.[53] Love can appear harsh and it can entail pain. Love does not always entail giving comfort to people, it can require that we take it away...

Think about it: when a parent berates their child for straying too far from the home, their anger could bring the child to tears but the parent does it out of Love, to keep the child from a greater harm which could come later. The same is true of many lessons taught by parents, priests, friends and family throughout life. Most of life's lessons are a small dose of pain which do us the

---

52 Genesis 19
53 John 2:15

kindness of growth. They are Love given to us by the people we meet.

The clearest way to express the place of pain and conflict in Christian Love is to realise that we do not show Love to someone by letting them carry out their evil. We can let others *persist* in their evil. After all, God does this by allowing us freedom. However, to let a murderer realise his thoughts unto the killing of an innocent... what Love have we shown him or his victim if we allow him to do this? If we know that a paedophile has abused children causing them untold harm; mentally, physically and spiritually, you may think it unloving to put this man to death... but how unloving is it to ignore his crimes and risk another victim? Indeed, if the execution of one paedophile meant that the next five would never commit their crime... then what?[54]

Even to a man who wants to claim that Jesus Christ is not our Lord and Saviour... we may allow him to express these thoughts but at the very least, we do this man no kindness by pretending that these thoughts are true, even if our denial of his position causes endless agitation.

Hence, we must always remember the common theme: that Love is often something that imparts a pleasant feeling but the pleasant feeling isn't necessary for Love. When we do good unto others, we are doing what is best for them whether that give pleasure or pain. I dare say that the majority of the Christian's moral life involves discerning what their Love entails. At which moments should we be gentle, which stern? Which moments require us to be warm, which cold? And which moments call for

---

54 And before we argue about whether killing is categorically wrong, note that in the original text the commandment is "thou shalt not *murder*" (Hebrew, *ratsach* (Exodus 20:13)). All murder involves killing, but not all killing is murder.

peace... or war? These question entail the conflicts of life but they all look to Love, the Will of God and joy to all mankind.

Printed in Great Britain
by Amazon